LEADERSHIP ASSETS

Empower your
Career
from the
Workshop
to the
Boardroom

Dr MONIQUE BEEDLES PhD

Published by Teak Yew Pty Ltd
Brisbane, Australia
Contact www.moniquebeedles.com

© 2021 Dr Monique Beedles

All rights reserved. Except as permitted under the Australian Copyright Act 1968, no part of this publication may be reproduced, stored in a retrieval system, or transmitted in any form or by any means, electronic, mechanical, photocopying, recording or otherwise, without prior written permission from the publisher. All enquiries should be made to the author.

Author: Dr Monique Beedles
Title: *Leadership Assets - Empower your Career from the Workshop to the Boardroom*
ISBN: 9780987191717
Subjects: Leadership | Career Advancement | Asset Management
Book production: www.smartwomenpublish.com
Book editor: Desolie Page, AE
Illustrator: Debbie Wood

 A catalogue record for this book is available from the National Library of Australia

Disclaimer:
The material in this publication is of the nature of general comment only and does not represent professional advice. All material is provided for educational purposes only. We recommend to always seek the advice of a qualified professional before making any decision regarding personal and business needs. To the maximum extent permitted by law, the author and publisher disclaim all responsibility and liability to any person arising directly or indirectly from any person taking or not taking action based on the information in this publication.

In memory of

My Grandad

William Beedles

a mechanic who became a barrister, but
always fixed his own Kombi.

CONTENTS

About The Author vii
Introduction. 1
To Lead 8
Chapter 1: A Whole-Of-Life
        Plan For Your Asset Management Career 13
Chapter 2: The Smarts You Need To Succeed. 27

LEADERSHIP ASSETS **41**

TECH SMARTS **43**
Chapter 3: Curiosity. 45
Chapter 4: Proficiency 61
Chapter 5: Ingenuity 75

BIZ SMARTS. **89**
Chapter 6: Mastery 91
Chapter 7: Tenacity 107
Chapter 8: Creativity 121

STREET SMARTS **137**
Chapter 9: Humility. 139
Chapter 10: Empathy 153
Chapter 11: Integrity 167
Case Studies .181
Next Steps 203
Tables And Figures 209

ABOUT THE AUTHOR

Dr Monique Beedles is an internationally recognised thought leader, bestselling author, and leadership coach who has built a successful career in asset management.

With more than twenty years of experience as a board director, and advisor to senior leaders, Monique has written *Leadership Assets* especially for asset managers who want to realise their leadership potential, and for leaders who want to empower their teams.

With a PhD in Strategy, a Master of Finance, and almost two decades running a successful advisory practice, Monique has defined her own success.

In *Leadership Assets*, she invites you to do the same.

INTRODUCTION

As a kid growing up, some of my earliest memories are of my Dad's workshop. We lived in a small town in rural New South Wales, where Dad sold and serviced motorbikes for the many farms in the area. Dad had built our house himself, on the back of the old town hall. New bikes were on show in the hall, and you walked through the workshop to get to our house.

The workshop was a wonderland of nuts and bolts, spanners and screws. The lingering smell of grease and oil hung in the air and all around were bikes pulled apart into myriad metal pieces, old and new. During those early years of my life, I more often saw machines in pieces, than in working order. I viewed them from the inside out. I understood that they were built by someone and therefore, could be fixed by someone.

Not far up the road, my Grandpop had what he called a 'shack'. It was his version of a workshop inside his house, just next to the kitchen, looking out over 500 acres of native bushland. Instead of motorbikes, Grandpop built electronics in his shack. Racks and shelves were lined with little containers filled with resistors, transistors, and LED lights of all kinds. The familiar smell was of melting solder and etching fluid. As kids we would work on projects with Grandpop, to build a bakelite box that made canary noises, or a toy car, with flashing lights. Grandpop had converted Gran's old foot-driven Singer sewing machine to electric power. Gran and Pop had also built their house themselves and there were always wires hanging loose on some not quite finished home improvement.

My Grandad, who was my Mum's father, had a garden shed. It was at the end of a short footpath that led from the back door of the kitchen, just past the clothesline, under the boughs of the mulberry tree. Along with nuts and bolts, it had fishing rods and flies and the salty, musty smell of well-worn waders. Grandad spent many evenings and weekends working on his Kombi. The Kombi always needed work. So much so, that he had a pit dug into his driveway, so he could just park the Kombi there and jump underneath it. No need for a jack.

I grew up believing that building things and fixing things was just what Dads do. Later on, in high school, I had a classmate whose father was a medical specialist. One Monday she told me that their washing machine had broken down over the weekend and that they'd called in a repairman. 'Why didn't your Dad just fix it?' I naively asked. 'My Dad doesn't fix washing machines,' she said. Until then, I didn't know that 'repairman' was a job.

It's perhaps no surprise then, that I feel at home in the world of asset management, with people who are passionate about building, fixing, and improving the world around us. But just as I'd never heard of a 'repairman', asset management wasn't a known career option when I was a kid. Over the past couple of decades asset management has matured as a professional discipline in its own right and this has opened up more well-defined career paths. However, many of these are still emerging, and as a multidisciplinary profession, there is no single career path for those working in asset management. Instead, everyone will have their own story of where they started out and what their ambitions are.

When he worked on his Kombi, my Grandad wore blue 'Stubbies' shorts and an old white singlet. It was a contrast to the black gown and white wig that he wore during the day, as a barrister, in Sydney. But Grandad hadn't always been a barrister. He grew up on the Wirral Peninsula in Northern England. His father had come across the River Dee from Wales. Grandad served in the British Army in World War II and shortly after that emigrated to Australia to play his part in the enormous post-war recovery and 'nation building' efforts. The ship landed him in Port Kembla, and he started his Australian life working as a fitter and turner at the Steel Works.

At that time, workplace health and safety was not what it is today. My Grandad had the misfortune to witness a workplace fatality, when a steel beam fell and crushed one of his workmates. He was subsequently called to appear in court, as a witness to the incident. During his time in the courtroom, my Grandad observed that 'these lawyers are no smarter than me'. This reflection prompted him to start studying law by night, as a *Student at Law* rather than at university, while continuing to work in his job by day.

His serendipitous experience, acute observations, definitive decision, and hard work, led to his later life as a singlet wearing, Kombi fixing, Macquarie Street barrister. Despite being able to afford a newer car, and to pay a repairman, Grandad continued to fix his own Kombi, for the simple joy of doing the work.

One of the most important things I learned from my Grandad is that your past doesn't determine your future. You can always pursue your dreams, if you're willing to put in the effort.

My own pathway in asset management has been far from conventional, but I think that as the 21st century rolls forward, there is no such thing as a 'conventional' career path. We each have our own unique story, and we each have enormous value to contribute.

At high school I loved maths and science, especially chemistry. As a teenager, my career ambition was to be the CEO of a global pharmaceutical company....in Switzerland. I wanted to help people by curing cancer, HIV, and as many other diseases as I could. Like many teenagers, I had small dreams....

When you have these kinds of ambitions, who do you turn to for advice? Nobody in my family had ever been to university. Neither of my parents finished high school. I didn't know any global CEOs and I'd never been to Switzerland.

With no source of credible advice, it seemed logical to me that to run a pharmaceutical company, I would need to study pharmacy. And so, out of high school that's what I did. It was always my intent to go on to honours and a PhD as a precursor to a career in industrial pharmacy. At some stage I would need to add an MBA, as I pursued a management track in the pharmaceutical industry. I also kept up my study of German at night school, because I figured I would need that in Switzerland.

I followed this path relentlessly, until the first year of my PhD studies in pharmaceutical sciences, where I went to the USA to present a paper at a top international conference. I was 21. At this conference I met many of the leading professors in my field, who talked about the younger generation who would follow in their footsteps—and had their eyes directly on me. I already knew that I didn't want to be a professor, or to pursue an academic career. I wanted to be out there in the world, making a difference.

I took a pause from my PhD and spent a year managing the sterile manufacturing facility in a large hospital pharmacy. I had also spent some time working in a pharmaceutical manufacturing plant, where I had learned, in a really practical way, about the impacts of machine design and reliability on operational performance. My German even came in handy with a particular German-built packing machine that, like the Kombi, was always breaking down.

I was then at a point where I had many options, but I needed to make a decision about the path I would take next. I could have given up on my PhD and gone straight on to an MBA. I had also spoken to the Dean of Engineering about a chemical engineering degree. He agreed to give me credit for 40% of the course, based on my previous studies. However, I still had my PhD scholarship and a deadline looming. These scholarships are highly sought after and not an easy thing to give away.

In exploring my options, I came to the decision to continue my PhD, but at a different university and in a different field. Business is multidisciplinary and those doing research in management come from many different backgrounds. There is no one undergraduate degree that feeds into postgraduate management studies. I embarked on my PhD in the School of Management in the focus area of Strategy, with the subject of my research in the global pharmaceutical industry. It brought together everything that I was interested in and meant I could draw on my background experience and learn deeply and richly to prepare me for the future I was seeking. I was told that it was like an MBA on steroids.

There will be many points in your career when you need to make a decision about which way to go next. You can take all the advice you like from people who are well meaning and want the best for you, but in the end, it's your own decision. There's no wrong choice, just different choices. It's up to you to make the most of whichever path you choose.

While undertaking my doctoral research, I continued to work part time in the hospital pharmacy, mostly at night and on weekends. Encouraged by my boss, I also took on my first board position. By this time, I was 25. When I finished my PhD, I spent a few years working and travelling overseas and figuring out my next steps.

Ultimately, in 2004, I decided to establish my own consulting practice. It was while working on strategy in the mining sector that I first came across the concept of asset management. I was working with what was then known as the 'Plant' department of a major mining company and quickly figured out that the management of their assets was critical to the success of their business. Having delved deeply into competitive strategy through my PhD studies, I understood that for them, asset management, done well, was a competitive advantage.

This led me to learn more about asset management, to undertake further training and to get involved in the Asset Management Council. From there I focused my work, still at the strategic level, in organisations where asset management was essential to their strategy. The more I explored asset management, the more I understood that it was also central to the strategy of the companies in my doctoral research, although we hadn't used that term. In those pharmaceutical companies, the most important assets were their patents. These intangible assets were the product of their capital investment, the source of their revenues, and their key competitive advantage.

Since then, I have established a niche practice, working with boards, executive teams and senior leaders in asset management. I provide team and individual coaching and one of the greatest rewards of my work is the "a-ha" moment, when those I'm working with have a breakthrough in their thinking that sets them on a path to success.

When I did well at school, my teachers encouraged me to become a teacher. Later, when I did well at university, the academics encouraged me to become an academic. In both cases, this was what success meant to them, but not to me.

People define success through their own perspectives, but their view of success shouldn't define yours.

What does success mean to you?

I'm passionate about seeing asset management on every board's agenda. I pursue this both by educating boards and senior leaders, and empowering asset management professionals to develop their leadership capabilities, to better engage with decision makers, and to become decision makers themselves.

My earlier book, *Asset Management for Directors* was written to give board directors and senior leaders an understanding of asset management. I've written this book, *Leadership Assets*, to give asset management professionals an understanding of leadership, to help you define your own success and to develop the smarts you need to reach your leadership potential.

I trust that it empowers you to confidently take your seat at the decision-making table.

Best wishes,
Monique.

TO LEAD

You make the decisions that matter.
The buck stops with you.
You want to do more than a job.
You want to create something that endures.
You want more than the corner office.
You want to be the cornerstone.
You understand that good ideas are nothing,
without decisive action.
You value integrity
and deliver on your promises.
You know that the decisions you make today
have consequences
for tomorrow.
You think ahead.

They don't make them
like they used to.
It's a throwaway society.

But you understand the joy
in caring for something of value.
You know that attention to detail
produces rewards.

The turn of a wheel
means everything,
to those who have honed their craft.
To plan for tomorrow,
is to value today.
To sustain that value,
creates the future.

Leaders connect people,
to bring ideas to the world.
Ideas that shape our human experience.
Leaders create connections,
to inspire change.
Great leaders
inspire the change
that shapes our world.

Leadership isn't easy.
You have tough days,
but you still show up tomorrow.
You have to carry your team,
no matter what pressure you're under.
You have to maintain your strength.
You need to look after you.
Resilience
means self-care.
'Once everything's back to normal'
- is a myth.

There's no going back.
There's a new kind of normal.
You need to make space for you
in your life,
to give you the strength to lead.

To lead takes Perspicacity:
Clarity of vision.
Penetrating discernment.
Insight
and Foresight.
An astronaut's view of the Earth.
An independent perspective.
Catalysis and Synthesis.
A fierce curiosity.
A deep understanding.
Question and
Listen.
A yearning for wisdom.
An ambitious future.
Learn and Grow.

You don't get to make the easy decisions.
They leave you with the curly ones.
There's no right answer,
but you do have to choose.
Vision brings clarity.
Purpose gives perspective.

Wise counsel
provides a clear road ahead.

To lead takes thick skin.
It will be lonely.
To lead takes courage.
You can't do it alone.
To lead takes judgment,
and you will be judged.
To lead takes wisdom,
and you will doubt yourself.
To lead is not an honour,
It's a responsibility.

To lead is to grow,
and to see yourself anew.

Monique Beedles 2012

CHAPTER 1

A WHOLE-OF-LIFE PLAN FOR YOUR ASSET MANAGEMENT CAREER

Asset management is a multi-disciplinary profession. There's no fixed pathway and no one place to start your asset management career. Many people are involved in asset management long before they realise it. You may be some way into your career already before you choose to pursue specialisation or professional recognition in asset management as a discipline.

Traditionally, asset managers primarily had engineering or trade backgrounds. However, as asset management has professionalised over recent years, and as international standards have been adopted with the recognition that asset management requires a whole-of-organisation perspective, it's increasingly likely that asset management professionals come from broader disciplinary backgrounds, such as accounting, finance, economics, information technology or human resources.

A trans-disciplinary approach improves the reach and impact of asset management, but it also requires a broader skill set beyond the technical fundamentals. No matter where you might be starting, having a whole-of-life plan for your career allows you to develop these skills from an early stage and to be proactive in building the capability you'll need to succeed in your chosen path.

I've defined four stages of career development in asset management: Apprentice, Advisor, Advocate, Ambassador. Let's see what each of these stages looks like.

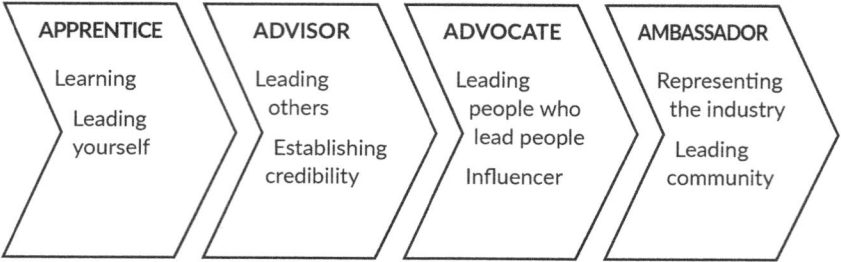

Figure 1: Four stages of career development

APPRENTICE

In the initial stages of your asset management journey, you'll be in the role of an Apprentice. This could be in a traditional trade through a formalised apprenticeship program. If so, you'll be working with an experienced tradesperson to learn the skills of your trade, while also undertaking formal training through a Vocational Education and Training provider. This combination of formal training and on-the-job learning enables you to develop both the theoretical and practical skills you'll need in your trade.

The Apprentice role is not just for trades though. If you're a new graduate fresh out of your undergraduate degree, you will probably take on a similar focus. Regardless of what field you've studied, it's likely you'll be part of a company graduate program, which generally run for one or two years. During this time, you'll be offered rotations in different parts of the organisation to help you gain exposure to the types of work you'll do in your professional role. You may also be involved in some in-house or industry-based training to ensure you have the baseline skills you'll need in your workplace.

You might also be an asset management apprentice if you've moved into asset management from a different professional background. You may be experienced in your technical area, but you're new to the discipline of asset management and to asset management roles. You'll likely have a lot of terminology to learn and there'll be language that has its own meaning in an asset management context. You might be in a new organisation, or in a newly established asset management team. You may have more experienced people to learn from and you may also undertake some asset management-specific training through an asset management professional body or specialist training provider.

From an asset management perspective, some of the key areas for learning at this stage are understanding risk, cost and performance and how they apply in your context. In an Apprentice role, you will focus mostly on technical risks that apply within your work, such as workplace health and safety and equipment failures. In terms of costs, you will most likely be focused on tracking operating costs, especially the costs of maintenance work. You'll be focused on your own performance and doing a good job within the scope of your role. You will need to work within assigned budgets and perform your work to expected timeframes.

Regardless of your specific role, being at the Apprentice stage is an exciting time as you accelerate along a steep learning curve. It's a time when you likely have nobody reporting directly to you. As you won't have any supervisory or managerial responsibilities, this is an ideal time to learn as much as you can, to try on different roles and to find what interests you. This is a time when you can afford to experiment, under close supervision, without being directly responsible for others. Make the most of this time to ask questions and seek advice from your more experienced colleagues.

It's never too early to find a mentor. Your period as an asset management apprentice creates opportunities to develop connections with more senior practitioners that will be valuable to you throughout your career. It's also a good time to get involved with the professional bodies in your industry or sector. Many such organisations will provide discounted rates for early career professionals as well as special events and mentoring or scholarship opportunities. Make the most of all these chances to build your networks, develop your skills and find your passion.

As an apprentice, you may be asking:

- What are the key skills I need to succeed in a career in asset management?
- Where should I start in planning my asset management career?
- Who should I look to for support?

In this initial stage, you are most likely to be primarily engaged in hands-on technical tasks. You are valued for your skills and your labour, in other words, *what you do*.

The key to successfully progressing through the Apprentice stage is to learn to lead yourself. Observing what others do is an important part of your learning at this stage. It's not enough, though. It's also important to observe what others say and how they behave.

Who are the leaders you admire?

What can you learn from them?

Have you seen examples of what not to do?

Even when you're just starting out, it's important to be looking ahead to the next stage of your journey and to be developing the skills you need for the role of an Advisor.

ADVISOR

As you move on from your apprenticeship and have a few years' experience, you may be offered your first opportunity to lead others. You may become a supervisor or lead a small team in your own trade or profession. It could also mean guiding a new apprentice or graduate in their early days within your organisation. Typically, in this stage you may have up to about 10 people within your spectrum of influence, either as a leader or an advisor.

With more experience, you may be a manager or a project manager, leading other experienced people who may each be specialists in their own areas. For example, as a maintenance manager, you may lead a group of complementary tradespeople, such as mechanics, electricians, or boilermakers. As a project manager you may oversee a range of specialists to deliver a specific outcome and be responsible for managing time and budgets. You are now in a situation where you don't necessarily share the same skill set as the people you lead. Your role is less about technical prowess and more about managing people.

At this stage you have well-developed technical skills, and you know your stuff. You're familiar with the established body of knowledge in your field and you will be called on by others for that expertise. If you don't have people reporting directly to you, you may be a consultant, advising clients external to your own company, or a technical specialist, advising internal stakeholders in your area of expertise.

As an advisor you're valued for your knowledge and expertise, that is, *what you know*.

At this stage you may want to seek professional recognition for this knowledge through asset management certification, such as the global certification programs accredited by World Partners in Asset Management, or through professional recognition within your specific field, such as engineering or accounting.

Some of the focus areas for development during this time are firstly around assurance. In a leadership role, you're no longer responsible just for your own work, but also for the work of others. This means you need to be able to demonstrate that you have systems and processes in place that provide assurance of the quality of work of your team. This includes being able to demonstrate that risks within your scope of responsibility will be identified, managed and escalated appropriately.

As an advisor, you'll need to move beyond a purely technical focus and beyond consideration of costs alone, to consider how the work of your team delivers value to your stakeholders. You may have some budget responsibility: you'll need to make decisions about how the resources allocated to you are best used.

As a leader, you'll need to consider alignment. How do you ensure that the work of your team aligns with your organisation's overall direction? How do you demonstrate that you are meeting specific objectives? Your role as a team leader or manager is firstly to understand how these objectives translate into your work context, and then to provide both the direction and motivation to your own team to work toward achieving them.

It may be the time when you begin to ask:

- How can I establish my credibility as a leader?
- How do I support my team to create value within our organisation?
- What capabilities do I need to develop to take the next steps in my asset management career?

Many people come to a point during this stage where they decide to pursue a people leadership pathway, with a view to moving into senior leadership and executive roles. Others may decide to specialise in a particular technical niche and may become leading experts in that area. Choosing one of these paths will take you on the journey to becoming an Advocate.

ADVOCATE

Once you have some leadership experience, you may move into a role where you now lead other leaders. You may have multiple managers, each with their own teams, reporting to you. In these senior leadership or executive roles, you may be leading dozens or several hundred people within your spectrum of influence.

You may also be in an Advocate role if you are a leading technical specialist in your field, even if you don't have as many people reporting to you directly. This role may also apply if you are a senior consultant or an independent professional in your own practice.

At the Advocate level, you are valued for your ideas and opinions: *what you think,* not just what you know.

Of course, nobody will know what you think if you don't share your ideas. This means that what you say becomes important. While this could be in the traditional manner of giving confidential advice to clients or internal stakeholders, it could also mean contributing your expertise more widely, through presenting at industry events, publishing papers and articles in relevant journals, or contributing in a leading role within your professional body or industry organisation.

At the Advocate level, you expand on solving known technical problems to leading innovation. It's time to go beyond the established body of knowledge and add your own ideas to create impact. It's no longer just about costs or a narrow view of value, but the wider and the more long-term effect you make through your work. Developing the skills to identify and measure that impact will help you to gain influence with a wider range of stakeholders.

As an advocate, your technical skills are not enough. You'll be expected to navigate increasingly complex social and political landscapes. You'll need to be savvy about how you engage with people outside your immediate group of colleagues. A strategic approach to developing your networks will strengthen your influence with a broader audience.

While Advocate is a term sometimes used in an adversarial setting, like a lawyer defending an accused criminal, advocacy is not just about defending yourself or others. More broadly it's about promoting your ideas and gaining support for proposals that can be seen in a very positive and beneficial sense. As a senior person you may be advocating for yourself, for your team, for your company, for your profession or for your industry, within the many contexts in which you operate.

It takes more than data to influence decision making. Maintaining a robust technical basis for your ideas is important, but the 'rational' argument is rarely enough. Learning the art of persuasion to expand your influence is an important capability at this level.

Some of the questions you may be asking yourself now are:

- How do I engage stakeholders across different disciplines?
- How do I improve my influence and impact?
- How do I get buy-in for innovative ideas?

Many people in technical fields will choose not to go down the path of leading people—it's not for everybody. If you do have the desire and the capability to be a leader of leaders, it can be a very rewarding journey. But it requires preparation and a commitment to continue to learn and grow throughout that journey. You will need humility, empathy, and integrity, some of the essential Leadership Assets that I'll talk about in this book.

AMBASSADOR

As an Ambassador, you may be a CEO, a non-executive director, or an elected representative in local, state or federal government. You may be in a senior role in a government organisation and a member of cross-sector committees, international bodies, or whole-of-government initiatives. You are leading thousands of people through your spectrum of influence.

As an ambassador, you are no longer working solely within your own organisation and with its stakeholders. Instead, you are active across organisations, and often across geographies and across industries.

Being an ambassador can place significant demands on your time and energy. Wide engagement may require evening and weekend events, extensive travel and dealing with the media. There's an old saying that 'You can't please all of the people, all of the time'. Ask any politician and they'll understand that at any given time about half of the people will disagree with them. That's a reality we need to accept when we step into a public leadership role.

Again, Ambassadorship is not for everyone, but there's a sense of reward in influencing the agenda on a wider stage. To succeed at this level, you'll need thick skin, a strong sense of purpose and robust personal integrity. You'll move from solely influencing others to being a person others want to influence.

At this stage, you're valued for your networks and your influence: *who you know* and *who knows you.*

Board roles will often highlight networks as one of the key criteria and may be seen as more important than knowledge or experience.

An ambassador is visible and leads by example. Leading by example is incredibly powerful. It's also challenging because others will look to you for consistency. For your own peace of mind, you want to maintain consistency between your own beliefs and the behaviours you repeatedly display. Inconsistency can be a barrier to credibility, as others observe the patterns of your behaviour. Developing routines and rituals is a way to embed consistency into your daily life and your work environment. These also contribute to developing desired cultures in your community. We'll discuss these further later in the book.

As visible leaders, you need to be committed to the vision and values of the organisation and communities you lead. If you're not committed to the objectives of the organisations you lead, how can you expect commitment from others?

You also need to be committed to your own health and wellbeing. When the going is tough and the stakes are high, it's easy to neglect your own self-care. One of my most important learnings from my time at Harvard Business School was that resilience is self-care. To consistently perform at a high level in high-stakes, high-pressure environments requires us to look after ourselves, so that we can better serve others.

A significant role for ambassadors is nurturing relationships. This goes beyond 'managing stakeholders' in a formal sense and relies on a proactive and personable approach to engaging with people and their needs. Ambassadors are conduits for collaboration: an important part of your role will be to bring people together and to provide opportunities for safe and open collaboration between potentially disparate groups who are working towards a common purpose.

At the Ambassador level you may be asking:

- How do I lead our community through uncertainty?
- How do I convey a clear message in complex situations?
- How do I maintain my own wellbeing when juggling multiple, demanding roles?

The challenges and rewards of an asset management career are lifelong. Wherever you are on your journey, there's always more to explore, as well as abundant opportunities for personal and professional growth.

Career Stage	Apprentice	Advisor	Advocate	Ambassador
Focus	Leading yourself	Leading your team	Leading your organisation	Leading your community
Spectrum of Influence	1 person	~10 people	100s of people	1000s of people
What you're valued for	What you do - your skills	What you know - your knowledge	What you think - your ideas	Who you know - your influence

Table 1: Asset management career stages

A successful career in asset management means a lifelong commitment to learn and grow, recognising that many of the assets you are responsible for may have a lifecycle that extends beyond your own lifetime. In the next chapter we'll explore the smarts you need to succeed on this journey.

CHAPTER 2

THE SMARTS YOU NEED TO SUCCEED

In the previous chapter, I mapped out a whole-of-life career plan for asset management professionals over four stages: Apprentice, Advisor, Advocate and Ambassador. At each of these stages, I mentioned some of the skills and capabilities required.

Just as we create whole-of-life plans for assets, a whole-of-life plan for our own careers provides a framework through which we can develop the necessary skills and capabilities needed throughout our careers. It's never too early to plan ahead and to focus your learning on your future ambitions.

I want to introduce three focus areas at each of the four stages I described in the previous chapter.

Focus Areas	Apprentice	Advisor	Advocate	Ambassador
Human	Performance	Alignment	Influence	Collaboration
Business	Cost	Value	Impact	Commitment
Technical	Risk	Assurance	Innovation	Consistency

Table 2: Focus areas at each career stage

These are areas of focus for your knowledge and skills development as you progress through your career. Even from the beginning, the capabilities you'll need span Technical, Business and Human spheres. Technical skills are necessary—but not sufficient—to progress into leadership roles.

Beyond knowledge and skills there are universal capabilities that are needed at every career stage. A mindful focus on nurturing these from early on will stand you in good stead throughout your whole-of-life career.

Tech Smarts underpin the solutions that create value and are delivered through your Biz Smarts. Making anything happen also requires Street Smarts.

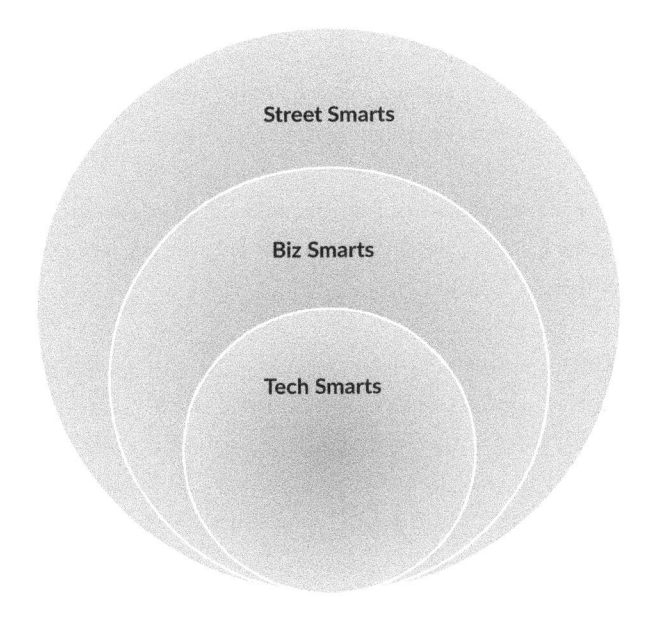

Figure 2: The smarts you need to succeed

These are the smarts you need to succeed!

Let's explore them further.

TECH SMARTS

Many asset managers I speak with feel frustrated that the decision makers in their company don't seem to understand the value of asset management.

They are struggling to get traction with executives or other leaders in the business and feel as though their work is not valued. This often means that they aren't being allocated the resources they need to implement effective asset management within their organisation.

While many executives may pay lip service to asset management, asset managers I speak with still feel in many cases that their CEO or their GM doesn't 'get it'.

When you have great technical expertise, it can be challenging to communicate concepts to people who don't have a similar technical background. Developing effective communication and engagement skills is essential to progression in your asset management career. We'll look at the importance of those skills a little further on.

Asset managers are excellent at identifying problems, analysing evidence and creating solutions.

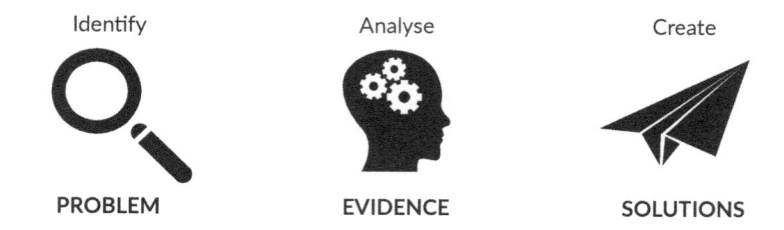

Identify	Analyse	Create
PROBLEM	EVIDENCE	SOLUTIONS

To make an impact, you have to meet a need. There has to be a problem to solve, even if those affected by the problem don't realise it. It's routine for asset managers to use an initial diagnostic step to identify that need and define the problem. Effective identification of problems relies on *Curiosity*, which we'll explore further in Chapter 3.

When solving a technical problem, we also need to understand the nature of the problem, which requires us to gather and analyse evidence. Asset managers have many tools at their disposal to analyse evidence—evidence can be as diverse as performance data, condition monitoring reports or financial statements. As an asset manager you can sometimes feel like a regular Sherlock Holmes, searching for clues and making deductions. *Proficiency* in analysing evidence is essential for asset managers: we'll explore this in Chapter 4.

Applying your Tech Smarts enables you to create a functional solution to an identified problem by analysing the available evidence. This requires applying your inherent human ingenuity, which has been honed through your technical training. We'll look at the importance of *Ingenuity* in Chapter 5. Coming up with a working solution may in many cases be relatively straightforward. Commonly, the greater challenge is to sell these solutions to a wider audience.

I have a friend from Austria who grew up skiing and snowboarding. When he came to Australia he had never been surfing before, but he found it easy to pick up. The body movements, muscle groups and basic balance skills needed for surfing are very similar to those needed for snowboarding, and he had already developed those.

It's similar with developing your smarts. The good news is that the capabilities you already have—to identify problems, analyse evidence and create solutions—can be applied beyond the technical domain to both the business and human contexts.

Your Tech Smarts will help you to develop your Biz Smarts and your Street Smarts.

The three core capabilities—to identify, analyse and create—are needed in each of these contexts.

Identify   **Analyse**   **Create**

You've developed these capabilities through your technical training and enhanced them through your ongoing experience. You've become a competent professional in your field. So you're already half-way there in developing those skills you need to become the person sought after and consulted for your technical expertise.

Applying these processes to developing your Biz Smarts and your Street Smarts will help you to influence decision makers. Beyond that, developing these smarts will help you to become a decision maker yourself and to progress into more senior leadership roles.

BIZ SMARTS

Even when you know that you have a fantastic technical solution, sometimes it's hard to gain the confidence to communicate that message. This can lead to considerable frustration, because you and your team have worked hard to create a solution that works really well, and you feel that your company won't get the full benefit from your effort if the solution is not implemented.

Developing your Biz Smarts will help you to feel more confident to pitch your ideas to decision makers. Building a convincing business case requires seeing your solution from the decision maker's perspective, rather than from the technical perspective alone.

In a business case, you need to identify a market, analyse business risks (not just technical risks), and create value for the organisation and its stakeholders.

Identify	Analyse	Create
MARKET	RISKS	VALUE

Taking these steps will augment your existing competence in your technical speciality, and give you influence with a wider business audience. Although decisions are made on behalf of companies and organisations, they are made by real people. Decision makers are human beings.

No matter how fantastic your technical solution is, you're going to need to persuade someone else. Unfortunately it's likely they don't have the same level of technical knowledge as you do. They probably won't recognise the intricacies of your technical case: how you've identified a problem, analysed the evidence and created a solution.

To build the business case you now need to identify a market for the solution you've created. You might already know what this is, but you may need to persuade others that the market is a viable one. If there's no market, there's no business case. You may have created a perfect technical solution, but if no one wants it, or is prepared to pay for it, there's no market for it. This principle applies not only in commercial markets, where you are selling a product to customers, but also to internal markets, where you are competing for funds or allocation of resources. *Mastery* to identify and understand potential markets is an essential business skill that we'll discuss in Chapter 6.

Once you know the market, you need to analyse the risks to the business in pursuing this market. You may have already identified the technical risks of your solution, but it's time to identify the business and strategic risks rather than solely the operational risks. To be viable, the value created needs to exceed the risks, or perceived risks, taken. It takes tenacity to carry on in the face of perceived risks. Rather than ignoring these risks, a robust approach to analysing and managing them is an essential leadership capability. We'll talk more about *Tenacity* in Chapter 7.

Ultimately, you need to be able to articulate how your solution creates value for the internal or external customer. Creativity isn't just for artists. Creative solutions that create value are essential to asset management and a key Leadership Asset. In Chapter 8 we'll talk more about what *Creativity* means in this context.

STREET SMARTS

Value is created through connections, not in isolation. You could have the world's most technologically advanced telephone, but if nobody else has a phone, who would you call?

Whether it's getting buy-in for a technical innovation or seeking your own job promotion, navigating the complexity of human networks and the prevailing political landscape requires Street Smarts. Beyond the technical solution and the business case, there is a human case, which is about creating meaning, not just financial value. It's important to understand who your stakeholders are and what is valuable to them. How does your work enhance that value?

To be Street Smart you first need to identify priorities. These are their priorities, not yours. You need to put yourself in their shoes when they ask, 'What's in it for me?' What imperatives are driving the decision maker? What are they rewarded for and how can you help them achieve their objectives? It takes humility to listen, to learn and to recognise the perspectives of others. We'll consider *Humility* more closely in Chapter 9.

When decisions are being made by a board or committee, there's more than one person you need to persuade. Considering the full range of perspectives around the table is a key to building a persuasive argument. Human connections are not random. Rather they can be analysed and cultivated to uncover and develop the human case.

Analysing the connections between you and key decision makers can help you to see the best path to take. What is important to them? Who influences them? Analysing connections is a key to becoming connected, rather than just consulted. Nurturing these connections to build relationships requires *Empathy*, an important attribute in developing these essential connections. We'll look into *Empathy* in Chapter 10.

Identify	Analyse	Create
PRIORITIES	CONNECTIONS	MEANING

As Aristotle wrote, persuasion requires a combination of ethos, logos and pathos. Logic and reason are usually not enough to persuade people. You also need to win their hearts and minds. Building on your technical skills to become more confident and convincing is a step-by-step process of taking what you already have and applying it to new situations.

To be valued for the role you play at every stage of your career, you need to go beyond creating solutions Your aim is to create value and ultimately, to create meaning for the communities you serve. Making meaning is what makes us human and that meaning can only be created in the context of connection with other human beings. It's a bit like an electrical circuit: electricity will only flow when the circuit is complete.

Alignment of values is essential to making meaning: the congruence between what you say and what you do will be observed by those you lead. Maintaining that congruence is the essence of *Integrity*, which we'll delve into in Chapter 11.

The Tech Smarts, Biz Smarts and Street Smarts I've outlined here are your Leadership Assets: you'll need them at every stage of your career.

	IDENTIFY	ANALYSE	CREATE
STREET SMARTS	HUMILITY Identify priorities	EMPATHY Analyse connections	INTEGRITY Create meaning
BIZ SMARTS	MASTERY Identify markets	TENACITY Analyse risks	CREATIVITY Create value
TECH SMARTS	CURIOSITY Identify problems	PROFICIENCY Analyse evidence	INGENUITY Create solutions

Table 3: Leadership assets required at every stage

LEARNING SMARTS

There's no need to wait till we are in a formal leadership role to work on developing these smarts. Rather, we start developing them before we've even begun our working lives. As students and lifelong learners, we continue to develop them throughout our careers and aim to continually improve our knowledge, skills and capabilities. This requires Learning Smarts, which are also essential to our leadership journey.

We develop our professional capabilities in three key ways:

- Formal training
- On-the-job learning
- Mentoring and coaching.

We often begin with formal training of some kind, whether it's university or vocational education and training through an apprenticeship or traineeship. Many of these options provide an initial exposure to on-the-job learning through industry placements and practical projects. When you start in a full-time role at the apprentice stage of your career, there'll be a period of rapid on-the-job learning. Learning this way continues throughout your life as you observe those around you.

Mentoring and coaching takes an individual approach to help you focus on your personal strengths and weaknesses, guide self-reflection and provide the perspective of an experienced person who has walked the path before you. This can augment formal training and on-the-job learning in a way that's tailored specifically for you.

Combining these three approaches provides you with the greatest depth of learning opportunities. Later, in Chapter 12, I'll present a series of *Case Studies* of asset management professionals at different stages of their career and how these three modes were effectively used in their own development.

Now, let's explore your *Leadership Assets*.

LEADERSHIP ASSETS

STREET SMARTS
- Humility
- Empathy
- Integrity

BIZ SMARTS
- Mastery
- Tenacity
- Creativity

TECH SMARTS
- Curiosity
- Proficiency
- Ingenuity

TECH SMARTS

CHAPTER 3
CURIOSITY

CURIOSITY

IDENTIFY PROBLEMS

For technically trained people, it can be easy to think that the main job is 'solving problems'. In maintenance-related trades this quite often means 'fixing things'. But before we can solve problems, we need to identify them.

Our natural human curiosity makes us well attuned to identifying problems: it's something we can all do. However, being great at identifying problems can mean that we see problems all around us and we can become overwhelmed by the number of problems that need to be solved.

The challenge is to channel our curiosity to identifying the relevant problems and to prioritise their relative importance so that we can solve the problems that most need solving. The worst thing we can do is put all our time and energy into solving the wrong problem.

Early in your career, the main problems you will likely need to identify are those related to technical risks. You'll be asked to find out 'what's wrong?' or 'what could go wrong?' Running any kind of diagnostic process requires you to be curious about finding anything that doesn't fit with what you have been trained to recognise as 'normal'.

When I was studying pharmacy one of the questions we asked our lecturers was, 'How will we know if a prescription is forged?' Their answer was, 'You'll just know!' At the time that wasn't a very helpful response, but it turned out to be true.

Late one evening at the hospital where I was working during my first year after graduation, I got a phone call from a man claiming to be a doctor and wanting me to issue injectable narcotics to a patient who was going to arrive at the hospital shortly. In a hospital, these drugs are issued routinely every day, so there was nothing unusual about the request itself. But every doctor knows there are strict protocols around the supply and use of these types of drugs and they wouldn't expect a pharmacist to breach these.

My curiosity led me to ask the caller a series of questions and, to me, his answers didn't add up. I wasn't convinced that he really was a doctor. It's not because I'd been taught what a person impersonating a doctor would say, but because through my training and my experience up till then, I knew what was 'normal'—how doctors spoke, the language they used, their manner and behaviours. So when I saw something that didn't fit that, my curiosity was piqued.

My curiosity led me to call the police who subsequently took the caller into custody. As I had rightly surmised, he was not a doctor. I later learned that he had a string of similar offences: I was not the first person he'd tried this on. Had I not been curious, the consequences could have been very serious. Our curiosity alerts us to anything out of the ordinary and helps us to identify where problems may lie.

As you progress through your career, the types of problems you need to identify will change. Early on, technical problems will be key. As you move into advisor and manager roles, business problems will become more important, as well as the problems your people are facing that you will need to deal with. As you lead a wider spectrum of people at a more senior level, you'll need to identify problems between teams and between organisations, including cultural and political issues.

At every stage, curiosity will be essential.

IGNORANCE IS NOT BLISS

We're told that 'curiosity killed the cat' and that 'ignorance is bliss', but we shouldn't really believe either of these. In truth, ignorance is not bliss and curiosity is the cure.

We're all born curious. Curiosity is the desire to learn, and it's as natural as the desire to eat. Just as a baby will cry until they're fed, so they will reach out to touch that colourful object or take a bite of that scrap they found on the floor. They just want to learn more about it.

Curiosity is essential to our survival as it alerts us to dangers and potential threats. If we're not curious about a roar from the trees, it may be too late once the lion has pounced. The flipside of this essential curiosity is the anxiety that comes from being ever alert to threats. At its extreme it can lead to paranoia and a crippling fear of trying anything new.

Ignorance is not bliss. Instead, knowledge is power. Rather than being afraid of the unknown, or defensive in the face of potential threats, a mindset of curiosity helps us to learn and to grow through the ever-changing uncertainties of life.

Dr Todd Kashdan, a professor of psychology, has done extensive research on curiosity. In his book *Curious?* he highlights five of the demonstrated 'big benefits' of being highly curious.[1]

Those with higher levels of curiosity show:

- improved health, including longer lives
- higher overall intelligence
- a greater sense of meaning and purpose in their lives
- healthier social relationships
- greater fulfilment and ultimate happiness.

While we're all born curious, our curiosity can decline if we don't nurture and encourage it. Since it's innate, we don't need to 'develop' curiosity. Rather, we need to avoid stifling it.

We know that three-year-olds love to ask 'why?' They'll ask it over and over again, never satisfied with an adult's perfunctory answer, driven by a compelling desire simply to know more. Sometimes the questions are impossible to answer, or too complex to explain to a three-year-old.

When my daughter was about this age, we were driving in the car and it was very quiet. Suddenly from the back seat she asked, 'Mummy, why don't Saturn's rings fall down?' I had no idea how to answer that. I've studied physics, but I'm not an astronomer and the reasons behind this are no doubt very complex. It's an interesting question, but outside my expertise.

Not wanting to stifle her curiosity, I had to admit that I didn't know that answer, but that we could try to find out—later, when I wasn't driving! Shutting down a question with a false answer or a guess won't encourage curiosity. Neither will killing it off with a response like 'That's a stupid question', or 'Why would you want to know that?'

There are no stupid questions.

When three-year-olds ask 'why?' they are following a natural instinct. One that's essential to their survival and growth. After repeatedly being told to 'be quiet' or 'stop bugging me', they give up asking.

The same thing can happen in the workplace if we don't have a safe space to ask questions. Sometimes we're afraid that asking a 'stupid question' will make us look incompetent. Instead, we should view questions as an indicator of a person's desire to learn—a desire that we should nurture and encourage.

If we're socialised to accept the status quo and 'not ask too many questions', our curiosity can be stifled as we move through life. To progress in your career, you need to actively nurture your curiosity and ensure it isn't suppressed. You need to develop a habit of always asking more, always probing deeper. A good question to ask yourself is, 'What else do I need to know?'

If your questions are being shut down or fobbed-off, look further. It may be that the real problem that needs solving hasn't been properly identified. In today's world, information is widely available and rapidly accessible. There's always someone you can ask.

We know that if we don't exercise, our muscles will atrophy. Likewise, nurturing your curiosity needs to become a habit. If you don't use it, you'll lose it. Asking questions and gathering information need to be part of your daily work. It's the way that you identify problems and it's an essential pre-requisite to solving them.

WHAT DOES A GOOD PROBLEM LOOK LIKE?

Not all problems are created equal. Some problems are big, some are small. Some are more important, and some are less important. Before we put a lot of time, effort and money into creating a solution for a problem, we need to ensure that the problem is worth solving.

I was once brought in to advise on a project to automate the time sheet adjustments for workers on the night shift on the two nights each year when the clocks are adjusted for daylight savings time, once forwards, then once backwards. Workers would be paid either too much or not enough, depending on which way the clock moved. The current system required a manual process to make the necessary adjustments to pay workers correctly.

The issue affected approximately six people, for two hours each year. By the time we finished the meeting, I calculated that the cost of the time for those present at the meeting was greater than the cost the company would incur by paying all six workers for an extra two hours each year. Pursuing this project for weeks, or months, engaging a software firm and making changes that would have knock-on effects into the whole time-keeping system would add significantly to the costs, which would far exceed the current administrative costs for the manual correction to be made. Was this problem really worth solving?

We can use standard risk assessment tools to prioritise both the importance and urgency of problems. This is useful in maintenance scheduling—understanding when critical breakdowns need immediate attention and when more minor defects can be scheduled for an opportune time.

These tools, however, rely on the problem being well defined and the parameters clearly specified. We need to understand the problem if we are going to prioritise action on the many problems that arise every day.

When we set out to define a problem, we need to channel our curiosity. What do we need to know to understand the problem well? It's very tempting to race ahead, developing a solution to what we think the problem is, before we have fully understood it.

A good problem should have three key characteristics:

- Specific
- Observable
- Open.

A good problem is specific

An ambition for 'world peace' is admirable, but not easy to action. It's too big and too nebulous to apply a workable process that will create a meaningful solution. A good problem is like a pin on a map: you know exactly where it goes.

Under the umbrella of a larger problem are smaller problems that we can define more specifically. For example, the problem might be 'climate change', but a better way to define a problem related to climate change could be to ask, 'How can we achieve net zero carbon emissions on our site in the next three years?' This may be just one in a series of climate change-related problems that you might choose to address.

A good problem is observable

If we did achieve world peace, how would we know?

Is climate change completely solvable, or just manageable? How will we know?

The whole field of radiology exists to 'show' us what would otherwise not be visible. An X-ray illuminates the problem in a way that looking at a person's skin can't. It's easier to solve a problem you can see.

When this problem is solved:

What will you see?
What will you hear?
What will you feel?
How will you know?

A good problem is open: it doesn't pre-empt the solution

Sometimes you see problem statements like 'How can we develop an app to improve community engagement?'

This statement pre-empts the solution. It pre-defines that an app is the solution to the problem. However, there may be many other ways to improve community engagement.

What do you mean by engagement? How is that measured? How will you know it has improved?

A more specific problem statement that doesn't pre-empt the solution might be 'How can we increase the number of people who use our public parks each week?'

Before you move onto the process of solving a problem, run a quick check to ensure it is specific, observable and open.

CURIOSITY EMPOWERS YOUR CAREER

Albert Einstein is reported to have said, 'I have no special talents. I am only passionately curious'.

Be curious about which problems are important

We need to be curious about which problems are important to our team, to our business, and to our careers. As much as we might like to, we can't solve all the problems at once. To empower your career, your curiosity needs to be channelled. It's easy to get carried away by things that are interesting (to you), but not relevant (to others). That doesn't mean though, that we should confine ourselves to the specific domain of our expertise. In fact, we can learn a lot by looking outside our domain to other companies, other countries and other industries.

I worked on my PhD in the late 1990s. There was email and there was internet, but certainly not the same rapid access to information that there is now. Some very recent research papers were available online, but most of what I needed was still in hard copy. To access research not held by my university's library required a request to another library, quite often overseas. A paper, photocopied from the original, would arrive in my in-tray in a big yellow envelope, usually about six to eight weeks later. I had plenty of time to be curious about what it might say. In that time, I pondered the question more deeply, found other relevant research, and asked more questions.

Curiosity drives innovation

Curiosity drives innovation, which is an imperative in today's economy. *New York Times* writer Ben Greenman highlighted what he calls 'productive frustration' as something the internet has quashed. Today we have access to so much information at our fingertips that we can satisfy our curiosity to know a specific fact in mere seconds. There's no time to wonder or to explore.

For my doctoral research I also had to analyse company annual reports, which I couldn't just download from their website, as we can today. As none of the companies I was researching were based in Australia, I needed to go overseas to access the British Library, the London Business School and other sources where these documents were kept. It made my research an adventure, not just an academic exercise, and it kept me curious.

Productive frustration, Greenman writes, allows questions to 'ripen, via deferral, into genuine interests'[2]. Just as we don't want 'spoilers' to tell us whodunnit when we're reading a mystery novel, instant answers deny us the 'pleasurable frustration of not knowing'.[2]

Productive curiosity goes both deep and wide to avoid taking the first readily available answer and instead, to ask more penetrating questions. Curiosity drives innovation, yet many company cultures stifle these very questions, while espousing the need to innovate. Professor Todd Kashdan studied workers in 16 countries and found that

> ...*while 65% said that curiosity was essential to discover new ideas, virtually the same percentage felt unable to ask questions*

on the job. The contradictions continued: while 84% reported that their employers encouraged curiosity, 60% said they had also encountered barriers to it at work.[3]

We know from experience that bureaucracy can be the enemy of curiosity. Many of us have metaphorically banged our heads against a brick wall trying to ask a simple question of a large organisation, only to be passed from one department to another by a seemingly endless stream of people who can't help us.

Be curious about how the bureaucracy works

Rather than give up in frustration, be curious about how the bureaucracy works. Understanding this complexity will help you to navigate it effectively and progress your career. Bureaucracy is a rule-based system. Pablo Picasso reportedly said that you need to 'learn the rules like a pro, so you can break them like an artist'. Ignoring the rules isn't the solution to the frustrations of bureaucracy: knowing the rules inside out allows you to use them to your advantage, without getting on the wrong side of the law.

Legendary Formula One designer Adrian Newey understood this well. Every year he relished poring over the new racing design regulations to work out what they actually said, as opposed to what their intent was. Given that his objective was to maximise the performance of the car, within the regulations, he would then ask himself, 'How can I use these regulations to try something that hasn't been done before?'[4]

Confirmation is a step in the process of gaining a PhD. This is usually about a year into the process, when you've reviewed the literature and spent time establishing your research question. There are documents to submit and presentations to give. Once your candidacy is confirmed, you can then move on with your research. When it came time for my PhD confirmation, I was very confident that it would go smoothly. I gave my presentation and was able to answer all the questions thrown at me from the pool of professors asking them. I submitted my documents paying careful attention to ensure that I'd met each and every requirement, including the instruction, printed in bold, which read **Do not provide a literature review**.

I was, unsurprisingly, devastated when my confirmation was denied, with the feedback saying that they would like me to **provide a literature review**. I didn't hide my anger and utter frustration and ended up in a teary mess in the pro vice chancellor's office, unable to understand why I was being penalised for exactly following their own explicit instructions. I was told by one of the staff in the office that it 'would make my research more robust'. My reply was that 'No. It would just make the paperwork more onerous'.

My supervisor advised me to take a legalistic approach and to 'throw their own rule book back at them'. After recomposing myself, I wrote a polite and precise letter to the powers that be, citing the university's written regulations and requirements that I had clearly followed. My candidacy was confirmed, and I progressed with my PhD. Being curious about how the bureaucracy works, rather than giving up in despair, helped me to move forward.

Be curious about other people's journeys

A catchphrase of advocates for women in leadership is that 'You can't be what you can't see'. Regardless of your demographic, role models can have a powerful impact. It's a lot easier to pursue a career path when you can see others that have journeyed the same way.

From role models and mentors we can learn both what's possible and what the potential challenges are likely to be.

I took on my first board role at the age of 25 and in a relatively short time I was a vice chair in a large organisation. As part of their succession plan, I was preparing to become the chairman. I had already completed the Australian Institute of Company Director's renowned Company Director's Course and as part of my preparation also completed their Chairman's Course. It gave some guidance from an experienced chair on such things as managing board dynamics and running meetings.

Added to this formal training and my experience as a vice chair observing the current chair in action, I also sought out some experienced chairs outside my own organisation, to ask their advice on the things I needed to be prepared for as a new chair. Being curious about other people's journeys helped to demystify the process and allowed me to take the next step with confidence.

I now mentor others who are taking the next steps in their careers, whether that be board roles, executive promotions or establishing their own enterprises. Being curious about other people's journeys helps me to guide mentees towards insights that empower them to confidently take that next step.

Being curious means identifying problems, but this doesn't apply only to the technical aspects of your work. You can apply the same curiosity to your own career journey, and you might be surprised where it could take you.

What are you curious about?

REFERENCES

[1] Kashdan, Todd. *Curious? Discover the Missing Ingredient to a Fulfilling Life.* New York: Harper Collins, 2009.
[2] Leslie, Ian. *Curious: the desire to know and why your future depends on it.* London: Quercus, 2014.
[3] Kashdan, T. *Companies value curiosity, but stifle it anyway.* Harvard Business Review, 21 October 2015.
[4] Newey, Adrian. *How to build a car.* London: Harper Collins, 2017.

CHAPTER 4

PROFICIENCY

PROFICIENCY

ANALYSE EVIDENCE

In the previous chapter I talked about the importance of remaining curious and asking pertinent questions to learn more. One of the things that can stifle curiosity is the fear of looking incompetent. Demonstrating competence is important but it shouldn't limit our learning.

After identifying the problem, we need to analyse the relevant evidence. We need to be proficient at analysing evidence before we launch into creating solutions. Evidence can quite often include data, but there are many other forms of evidence too. Proficiency in analysing evidence means we need to understand what kind of data is valuable. The way we frame our problem must consider the types of data to be analysed for both diagnosis and problem solving.

CULTIVATE INSIGHTS

We need to be proficient at analysing evidence, but it's not just about crunching numbers. It's the insights we gain, not the data itself, that are important for problem solving and decision making. Beyond analysing data, we need to cultivate insights.

Cultivating insights is different to preventing mistakes. Focusing too closely on finding faults and putting all our energy into preventing mistakes can blinker us to the insights that surround us. Gary Klein, a cognitive psychologist, characterises performance improvement as having two components: Reducing Errors + Increasing Insights.[5] Both are needed to see performance gains.

Yes, reducing errors and mistakes is important, but if it's the only thing you do, you'll return to baseline, without making any positive gains. For that, real insights are required.

While in-depth data analysis may be a highly technical skill, everyday insights are more common than we think. Our brains are hard-wired to seek patterns and meaning. This is quite often a subconscious, rather than a deliberate process. In fact, just like focusing on preventing mistakes, trying too hard to solve a problem can sometimes block the process of gaining true insights. We've probably all had the experience of trying really hard to think of something without success, only to have it suddenly jump into our minds while we're walking the dog or taking a shower.

In his book, *Seeing what others don't: the remarkable ways we gain insights*,[5] Gary Klein describes three ways that insights can emerge:

Firstly, insights can come from seeing a *pattern* among apparently disparate evidence, joining the dots between repeated observations. Such a pattern can reveal an underlying truth. It's like the chorus of a song, it keeps coming back over and over, but it ties the verses together.

Secondly, insights can come from *combinations*, linking seemingly unrelated ideas to come up with something completely new. This is a bit like grafting two species of plants to create a new fruit or vegetable. The lemonade tree is a cross between a lemon and a mandarin: it creates a fruit that has a lemony freshness, without the strong sourness of a lemon alone. Perfect for freshly squeezed lemonade or just for eating straight from the tree!

Thirdly, insights can come from *inconsistencies*, where we recognise that some of the evidence doesn't fit or is out of place. When we identify an inconsistency we're drawn to resolve it. Seeking either the cause of the inconsistency or the method to resolve it can lead to further insights. It's a bit like a pothole on the road. When you're driving along smoothly and there's suddenly a bump and a noise you didn't expect, it indicates an inconsistency in the road surface and alerts us to something that requires our attention.

In 2020, an optometrist in Adelaide was convicted of fraud and had his professional registration withdrawn, after deliberately altering more than 400 spectacle prescriptions made by a colleague.[6] This tampering occurred over a long period of time and had led his colleague to question her own professional competence, after dozens of patients returned with incorrect prescriptions.

The insight that led to the discovery of this tampering required all three of the processes Klein described. Inconsistencies led patients to return their glasses, as they couldn't see properly with them. Over time, a pattern of these inconsistencies led to the matter being investigated. Thankfully, the prescribing optometrist kept her own meticulous records. Combining information from these with forensic examination of computer system logins showed that it was not the fault of the optometrist who had written the prescriptions, but rather her colleague who had deliberately altered the details.[7]

While the optometrist charged initially had his licence suspended for 12 months, on appeal it was extended to a 5-year suspension.[8]

Analysing data is important, but it's often not sufficient in itself to provide the insights we need. There is a role for intuition and 'trusting your gut': when something doesn't look or feel right, it's time to pause and investigate further, which may well mean seeking more data or further evidence to support or quash your hunch.

THE DEVIL IN THE DATA

A few years ago, I bought a new set of golf clubs. The golf pro asked me about my game, and about where I would like to improve. Naturally I told him that I wanted to improve my score. He explained how different clubs could help different areas of my game to achieve this.

The golf pro then surprised me by saying, 'Most customers who come in looking for new clubs all want the same thing—to hit the ball further. None of them ever say that they want to improve their score'.

Golf is a multifaceted game. Just hitting the ball further might look impressive, but it won't necessarily improve your score and help you to win the game.

At each stage of a golf game, you have to decide:

Will I use the driver or the three iron?

Should I try to hit over the water hazard, or go around it?

How fast is the green and how hard do I need to putt?

You can buy the biggest driver on the market and proudly step up to the tee and hit the ball right onto the green in one shot. But if your putting is terrible, you can still end up with an average score and a poor performance.

Hitting the ball further is just one tactic. The strategy of a good golfer will include many other tactics, carefully chosen at the appropriate time to meet the overall objective—achieving the best score possible and winning the game.

Like the golfer who only wants to hit the ball further, many companies focus on the big-number figures like revenue, turnover and sales—even 'work-in-hand'. They sound impressive: the bigger the number, the better it must be.

But those who focus only on these measures are trying to hit the ball further without improving their score. When we analyse data, useful insights rely on asking the right question and measuring the right thing in the data we've chosen to examine.

We've spoken about cultivating insights. It's important that our approach to analysing evidence supports these insights, rather than undermining them. If we're to be proficient in our analysis of evidence, we need to avoid limiting our intuitions. Let's look at some of the ways in which we can actually constrain, rather than cultivate, insights.

Ronald Coase, a Nobel Prize-winning economist, said, 'If you torture the data enough, nature will confess to anything'.[9] The 'race to model' at high speed can undermine valuable insights if predictive models are built without fundamental understanding. It's like a building without a solid foundation. We shouldn't be in a hurry to draw the first conclusion that we see from data in any context. Instead, we need to understand what it is, where it's coming from and what it means.

In today's 'big data' world, the volume of data can be overwhelming. In asset management, nearly everything has a sensor on it these days, pouring out seemingly endless rivers of data. What do we do with it all?

Douglas Merrill, a former CEO of Google, has said that with too little data, you won't be able to make any conclusions you trust, whereas with too much data, you'll find relationships that aren't real.[10] While we all know that correlation is not causation, it's easy to fall into the trap of making false connections between parameters when we are overwhelmed with the volume of data.

Sampling errors and auto-correlation can occur when there's a poorly managed large pool of data. Enormous resources can be wasted when proficiency in the skills and systems needed to make sense of the data is lacking. There's a world of spurious statistics, where false conclusions can be drawn between completely unrelated items. Tyler Vigen, a Harvard statistician, runs a website called *Spurious Correlations* for a humorous take on how data can be misused. For example, the number of people who drown by falling out of a fishing boat correlates to the marriage rate in Kentucky (R=0.95). You can find more of these and their pictorial representation at www.tylervigen.com/spurious-correlations.

Avoiding the perils of dubious data in order to create value and meaning instead requires a grounding in the context. On my latest trip to the UK, I spent a day visiting Bletchley Park, the secret codebreaking headquarters during World War II. One of the keys to the success of codebreaking is a process called traffic analysis. This is a basic part of signals intelligence and is based on analysing the patterns of communication, independent of the message itself.

Factors such as when, from where, and by whom messages were sent was relevant to decoding their meaning, independent of what the message might say. A weather report in summer is unlikely to include snowfall. Keeping messages in context narrowed down the possibilities when it came to breaking codes. All incoming intercepts were meticulously logged and cross-referenced to build up a picture of the signals incoming from all directions. Invalid data could then be excluded, and erroneous interpretations avoided. This made the codebreaking process much more efficient, which was important in a situation where time was of the essence. It wasn't enough to break the code eventually: it had to be broken in time for practical action to be taken on the de-coded message.

While there's a lot of focus on the importance of coding skills, we learn from Bletchley Park that de-coding is as important as coding. Analysing evidence is not just about data gathering, but about de-coding to create meaning. We need to be concerned not just with the accuracy of data, but with its veracity—in other words instead of asking, 'Is it correct?' we need to ask, 'Is it true?'

What truths does your data reveal and how can you ensure that you are best placed to uncover those truths?

SHOW WHAT YOU KNOW

Developing your proficiency in any skill requires deliberate effort. In the early stages of your career, building your technical skills is important so that you're competent to do your work. Some will be developed on the job, but other skills will require further formal training, both to learn them and to keep them up to date.

If you want to improve your fitness, an exercise physiologist will first assess your current fitness level. They will probably look at various body measurements and test your speed and strength through a range of exercise tests. They'll note these data as a baseline for you to commence a fitness program and they'll prescribe an exercise regime based on their assessment of your current fitness and your goals.

The process is very much the same when looking to develop your work-related skills and proficiencies. Assessing your current ability level, identifying your goals, then devising a program that will take you from where you are now, to where you want to be in the future. This program can involve a combination of taking on more challenging tasks and projects, seeking higher level roles, undertaking formal training, self-reflective practice, and coaching or mentoring.

Understanding what proficiencies you need is a key part of this puzzle. At each stage you need to be working on the skills you'll need at the next level, not just at the level you're working at now. It's never too early to develop those attributes you will need down the track. When I was first in the position of vice chair of a board and being positioned to take on the chair role, I went through a deliberate process of assessing what skills I would need to do that well. I undertook formal training relating to the role of the chair and I sought out experienced chairs to ask their advice. I also got on-the-job training as the current chair allowed me to shadow him in his role to 'learn the ropes'. All of these combined to help me to feel confident to step up when I later took on my first chairman's role.

It's not enough to be proficient, you also have to demonstrate that proficiency. Within the asset management profession, a globally recognised competency framework, such as that provided by World Partners in Asset Management, helps you to understand what competencies are required at each level and how these can be demonstrated through qualifications and experience. Industry frameworks such as this can be used in combination with those that might be specific to your discipline, such as engineering, finance or a trade. Looking to these types of external validation of your competencies is useful for both internal promotion and credibility beyond your organisation. Addressing these external requirements in parallel with your organisation's own internal development frameworks and programs will give you flexibility and choice as your progress along your desired path.

Most leadership and competency frameworks have a step-wise approach that allows you to make progress throughout your career over a series of levels. It's wise not to leap ahead too quickly, but to take the time to demonstrate your capability at each level before moving on to the next step. I've worked with people who wanted to step up into higher-level responsibilities before they had demonstrated their ability to carry out simple tasks in a proficient and timely manner. The reality is that demonstrating competence, even in low level tasks, is an important part of building the trust that leaders need to allocate higher levels of responsibility. If you can't demonstrate that you can do a simple task well, you won't be trusted with something more complex.

By the same token, nobody wants to be held back in a mundane role when they are capable and ready for something more. If you aren't visible in demonstrating your capabilities, you may be overlooked for desirable opportunities. So it's important to have open and honest dialogue with your leaders so that they are aware of your goals and the opportunities you're open to. A good leader won't be threatened by this, because they'll understand that to keep good people, they need to ensure they are engaged and see a viable and positive future within the organisation. A leader who stifles your growth is not one you would likely remain with for long. Don't wait to be asked to step into new roles—or to receive the proverbial tap on the shoulder. Step up and offer to take on more responsibility when the time is right for you.

Your workplace is not the only opportunity to demonstrate your proficiency and leadership capability. Explore the many opportunities outside of your paid work where you can take on higher levels of responsibility, learn leadership skills and demonstrate your capabilities. Volunteer for leadership roles in your professional body, school committees, alumni organisations, or your local sporting club. Offer to mentor others or seek a mentor in the schemes offered by these organisations. You'll develop skills and confidence, expand your networks and maybe even find your next job offer.

If you're fortunate enough to have an employer that supports your professional development by funding formal training, providing an internal or external mentor, giving you opportunities for step-up responsibilities, or on-the-job learning, then you should make the most of what's available. When you attend a conference or external training, there's so much that you bring back to your role. It's a great idea to actively share what you've learned, both to maximise your learning, and to demonstrate the value created for your team in having people participate in the conference or training. Think about providing a 'lunch and learn' with a short presentation, a newsletter piece, a video, or another formal or informal opportunity to share so that everyone can gain something from your experience.

While in the early stages of your career, the evidence you analyse may primarily be technical, the skills of understanding context and prioritising for meaning will be increasingly important as you move into leadership roles and apply these same skills to more complex business and political problems. We're always building on our knowledge and skills, never abandoning what we know; rather we carry it forward and integrate it into who we are and what we have to offer.

REFERENCES

[5] Klein, G. *Seeing what others don't: The remarkable ways we gain insights.* London: Nicholas Brealey, 2014.

[6] Siebert, B. "Adelaide optometrist struck off register after tampering with hundreds of glasses prescriptions", *ABC News*, 13 September 2020.

[7] BBC report. "Australian optometrist suspended for altering prescriptions", *BBC World News*, 13 September 2020.

[8] Boisvert, E. "Optometrist who altered hundreds of glasses prescriptions has ban increased to five years", *ABC News*, 13 May 2021.

[9] Coase, R. *How Should Economists Choose?* The Third G. Warren Nutter Lecture in Political Economy, Washington D.C.: American Enterprise Institute for Public Policy Research, 1982.

[10] Merrill, D. "RIs Not Enough For 'Big Data'", *Forbes*, 1 May 2012. [Online]. Available: https://www.forbes.com/sites/douglasmerrill/2012/05/01/r-is-not-enough-for-big-data/?sh=18c6e0f25924

[11] World Partners in Asset Management, "Global Certification Scheme", 2021. [Online]. Available: https://www.wpiam.com/global-certification-scheme/

CHAPTER 5

INGENUITY

INGENUITY

CREATE SOLUTIONS

In the 1990s the pharmaceutical industry was in the midst of a biotech boom. Recombinant DNA technologies and biological pharmaceuticals brought novel treatments to previously untreated conditions. For my PhD I researched the top 21 global pharmaceutical companies, who together represented a discrete strategic group. By the end of my four years of research there were 14 companies left. A flurry of merger activity between the dominant players in this industry was driven by the imperative for innovation.

A pharmaceutical patent lasts 20 years. It can take 15 years for development from the stage of patent registration to a final product on the market. These companies then have about five years to make a return on the multi-billion-dollar capital invested in the process. Therefore, they need a steady pipeline of new patents coming through to maintain their competitive advantage. They need to remain innovative, while maintaining efficient production and distribution networks on a global scale.

These competing imperatives can be challenging to manage. One way pharmaceutical companies do this is to create strategic alliances with small start-ups and university research labs through joint ventures, licensing arrangements or direct acquisition. What I found through my research on the performance of these companies over a ten-year period, is that those companies who focused on acquisition as their key strategy grew faster in the beginning, but those who instead focused on nurturing an innovative culture from within, had more sustainable growth over the long term.

In the 1990s pharmaceuticals was an ideal example of an industry with an imperative to innovate.

In the 21st century, every industry has an imperative to innovate.

The imperative for innovation in every sector has never been greater. Asset management is a risk-based discipline and often the imperative to manage risk can compete with the imperative for innovation.

Asset managers can balance these competing imperatives by taking a risk-based approach to innovation. This approach increases the likelihood of success, while limiting the consequences of failure. De-risking innovation requires collaboration, consistency and commitment.

DON'T BE A HERO

In Western society, there's a myth about the hero scientist—Newton being struck by an apple, Archimedes leaping from the bath exclaiming 'Eureka!' While there may be grains of truth in these stories, great achievements are rarely made by individuals acting alone. In reality it takes a team and active collaboration to make significant breakthroughs.

For example, the discovery of the Higgs Boson particle took nearly 50 years and the input of thousands of scientists. The Large Hadron

Collider used for this work likewise involved thousands of scientists and engineers and took 10 years to build.[12]

In 2011 my husband and I enjoyed our honeymoon in France. We were lucky enough to follow the last four stages of the Tour de France, through the French Alps and the legendary Alpe d'huez, onto the streets of Grenoble for the time trial, and into Paris for the grand finale on the Champs Elysée. That year Cadel Evans became the first Australian to win the Tour de France. We cheered and yelled, drank champagne, waved our Aussie flags and sang along to 'Advance Australia Fair' with Tina Arena.

My husband and I are not cyclists, but for years we have been captivated by the Tour de France and had spent countless late nights following the progress of Cadel Evans and his Tour de France dream. In sporting terms, this is a fantastic achievement. On his homecoming in Melbourne, crowds filled the streets to shower accolades on one man and his bicycle. But behind the scenes in France, we had seen the sheer scale of the operations that go into making this race possible. Millions of people, billions of dollars. The Tour de France is not won by one man and his bicycle, but by a huge team, all dedicated to the same dream.

What can you create together that you can't create alone?

The status quo doesn't shift because you're right

In his book, *This is Marketing,* Seth Godin highlights that if all it took to upend the status quo was the truth, we would have changed a long time ago. The status quo only shifts when the culture changes.[13]

A good example of this is smoking in public, which was once commonplace and socially acceptable. The detrimental health effects had been known for decades. There was no lack of evidence to support quitting smoking for individuals or banning smoking in public for collective community health. Gradually bans came into force and bit by bit the social acceptability of smoking was eroded. Now, even smokers don't like others smoking around them. Despite the readily available data and evidence against smoking, social exclusion is a stronger motivator than potential future health risks, which seem less tangible.

If you're trying to implement a solution that you know will have great benefits, it's not enough to be technically right. Beyond the technical case, you need to make the business case and the human case. Collaboration is key to understanding the needs of your stakeholders and implementing the most effective strategies to deliver change.

It takes 20 wickets to win a test match

As a kid my summers were filled with cricket. We watched games on TV and then we'd play cricket at the beach or in the backyard with a transistor radio going so we didn't miss a ball. Some of my earliest memories are of fast bowlers Lillee and Thompson pounding the pitch against the Windies (that's the West Indies) and batsman Allan Border smashing it out in the Ashes (the trophy for the victors in the Australia v England test matches).

My young daughter loves to watch cricket and over time she's learning its nuances. This week when she saw a score displayed as 7/103, she asked, 'Mummy, which number do you pay attention to, the 7 or the 103?' Of course, you can't look at either number in isolation.

For the batting team it's a delicate balance between the runs you need and the wickets you have in hand—how much risk you need to take versus how much risk you can afford to take. Defensive play might eke out a draw, but to win, you have to take some risks.

Later, in the chapter on *Empathy*, I outline some of the ways we can make collaboration more effective, as part of a low-risk approach to innovation.

ROUTINES FOR SUCCESS

Consistency and creativity aren't mutually exclusive. We often think that rigorous processes will stymie innovation, but in fact, most creative pursuits require a disciplined approach.

Barack Obama favoured blue or grey suits during his time as President. As he said to *Vanity Fair*, 'I'm trying to pare down decisions. I don't want to make decisions about what I'm eating or wearing. Because I have too many other decisions to make'.[14]

Our brains have limited bandwidth for processing information, and decision-making chews it up, leaving less capacity for other thinking. It's like being in a traffic jam. The road has limited capacity, only one vehicle per lane. Even on a multi-lane highway, an accident or breakdown will force the rest of the traffic behind it to slow down. There's no way around it. You have to clear the obstruction to keep the traffic flowing.

While building routines may seem a counter-intuitive way to create opportunities for innovation, the paradox is that routines reduce our cognitive load, effectively automating trivial decision making to free up our brain space for more important thinking.

Consistency, along with commitment and collaboration, is central to reducing the risks and uncertainty of innovation initiatives. Introducing routines, such as a regular scheduled time for specific activities, builds consistency to improve the chances of success.

What routines do you and your team have in place and how do they improve your work?

Rituals build consistency

John Buchanan was coach of the Australian cricket team during one of its most successful periods. In his book, *If Better is Possible*, he describes the ritual of presenting a new test player with their baggy green cap as a 'sacred act': 'The cap is always given to a new player by a former player in a small team ceremony at the warm-up huddle on the day of the new player's debut. While every presentation is significant, the older the player who presents the cap, the greater the link to the legions of players who have gone before.[15]

As John explains, 'The baggy green cap is the ultimate symbol of the Australian cricket team. It is to cricket what the slouch hat is to the fighting spirit of Australian troops. It embodies all the heroes, epic battles, awards and the individual and team records, but more than that, it captures an inner spirit which sees Australian teams play with aggression, skill, innovation, dominance and never-say-die attitude. It is what backyard and schoolyard dreams are forged upon'.[15]

Rituals exist in every human society. Whether in religion, the military, sport, universities, or in a simple handshake, rituals are all around us. They can reduce our anxiety, improve our performance and help us to feel we belong. Rituals build consistency and stability, and help us to feel safe. This safety of belonging settles our 'fight or flight' response and empowers us to perform at our best.

Part of the reason that the baggy green is so special is that each player gets only one. They are individually numbered and a player wears the same cap throughout their career. That's why when Shane Warne (an outstanding bowler 1992–2007) chose to auction his baggy green to raise funds for bush fire relief, it was a big deal. The cap fetched over one million dollars, an indicator of the cultural importance of the baggy green well beyond the dressing room walls.

Routines free up our working memory, by automating a process so we don't have to think about it. Instead, it's done almost unconsciously. By contrast, a ritual demands our attention. It is heavy with meaning and symbolism. It focuses our consciousness and consumes our working memory, leaving no space for concern with the trivial. Both routines and rituals are important to developing the consistency needed for successful innovation.

What rituals do you have in your team?

What do you do to help people feel that they belong?

MAKE A COMMITMENT

It's easy to say that you're innovative. It's easy for companies to have an 'innovation' pillar in their strategic plan, to insert a paragraph on innovation in their annual report, or even to list innovation as one of their values, but what does true commitment to innovation look like?

At least three types of commitment are required for effective innovation: financial commitment, time commitment and cultural commitment.

Financial commitment

Part of the perceived risk of innovation is that 'we can't afford it'. Some fear that costs will spiral out of control. While the outcomes of specific innovation initiatives are, by definition, unknowable, the costs can and should be well defined and clearly controlled. A financial commitment to innovation should be clear in the budget, where specific funds have been allocated to innovation initiatives.

Defining your financial commitment helps to reduce risk, by employing the concept of affordable loss. Just like any other budget item, funding for innovation should not be a bottomless pit. Allocate what you can afford and put those funds to best use. Like a bungee rope, this allows you take the plunge while at the same time feeling secure that there's a limit to how far you can fall. Setting budgets limits the downside risk, without restricting the upside opportunities that innovation brings.

A lot can be achieved even with a small investment. It's the commitment itself, rather than the size of the budget that's important. However, even a small amount of money will be wasted if there isn't also a commitment of time and a cultural commitment by the organisation.

Time commitment

On our honeymoon in France, my husband and I visited Monet's garden at Giverny. It's a beautiful French country house, every room in a different monotone palette. Monet loved colour and his studio looked out over the garden. He built a lake, complete with a bridge, and planted his famous gardens, just so he could paint them.

We understand that an artist needs time and space to be creative. Nobody expected Monet to pop out a masterpiece between meetings. Yet in so many organisations, people are expected to 'be innovative' in and around their usual day jobs, with all its pressures and moment-to-moment decisions. Allowing people time for creative thinking is an important part of an organisation's commitment to innovation. Whether that's time alone for deep reflection, or time together for collaborative problem solving, innovation requires allocated time and dedicated attention.

People's time comes at a cost, which can be particularly challenging if your business model relies on billable hours. Sometimes it's the business model itself that needs innovating. Like financial commitment, your time commitment should be within your resources. Innovation should not add to the endless pile of work people already have to do. If so, it will become a chore, and the required creativity will be lacking.

How are you making the commitment to time for innovation in your business?

Cultural commitment

A crash diet can help you to lose weight quickly, but it's common for people to regain that weight, and more, when they go back to eating normally. Crash diets are extreme, and not sustainable. Instead, a sustainable approach to healthy eating requires a long-term commitment to make more healthy choices every day.

It's the same with innovation. Companies can 'buy-in' their innovation through acquisitions, mergers and licensing agreements, but a more sustainable approach is to build a culture of innovation from within. My doctoral research investigating the link between a company's strategic decisions and their long-term profitability, showed that those companies who chose to 'buy' their innovations primarily through acquisition, initially grew more quickly, but like a crash diet, their performance wasn't sustainable over the long term.

Instead, those companies who chose fewer mergers and strategic alliances, in favour of nurturing an internal culture of innovation, performed better over the 10 years of my study and are now some of the world's most successful companies. Gordon Binder, former CEO of AMGEN, one of these high performing companies, describes some of the keys to developing a culture of innovation and growth in his book *Science Lessons*. He emphasises to be generous with praise, time and attention, and to share credit freely. This approach costs nothing, but it is essential to attracting and retaining the people who are at the heart of any innovative culture.[16]

Committing to a culture of innovation means accepting that there are no bad ideas. There are no bad cards in a deck: it's what you do with them that determines the outcome. Certainly, ideas may require further development, but formative ideas are the basis for further new ideas. Dismissing ideas up front, without allowing them to be developed, risks overlooking the enormous potential of our human ingenuity.

REFERENCES

[12] Morgan, J. "Higgs boson scientists win Nobel prize in physics", *BBC News*, 8 October 2013.

[13] Godin, S. *This is Marketing*. London: Penguin Random House, 2018.

[14] Lewis, M. "Obama's Way", *Vanity Fair*, no. October 2012.

[15] Buchanan, J. *If Better is Possible*. Melbourne: Hardie Grant Books, 2007.

[16] Binder, G. & Bashe, P. *Science Lessons: What the business of biotech taught me about management*. Boston: Harvard Business Press, 2008.

BIZ SMARTS

CHAPTER 6

MASTERY

MASTERY

🔍 IDENTIFY MARKETS

As a frequent flyer, I've often waited in the pre-dawn darkness for my cab to the airport. It's always good to know what the weather will be in your arrival city. These days, it only takes a moment to swipe your phone and find out. On a recent trip to Canberra, I grimaced when I saw that it was -4.7 degrees Celsius in the capital (feels like -7.7!). However inconvenient for a Queenslander, I had no hesitation in carting my winter coat, gloves and scarf, because I knew I would need them.

Prior to the 1840s, the concept of a weather report didn't exist. The transmission of information was so slow that by the time weather information arrived, it was too late for it to be useful. Weather was largely a surprise.

That all changed with the introduction of the electric telegraph. For the first time, people had what James Gleick describes as 'some approximation of instant knowledge of a distant place'.[17] They could be warned, for example, that rain was coming from the north, before it rained. The idea was transformative and by the 1850s governments had begun to establish meteorological offices.

Value is created only when a need is met. Weather information has little value if the weather has already passed. Since the purpose of asset management is to create value for stakeholders through assets, then as asset managers part of our core work is to identify opportunities to create value. This means we need to identify markets. These need not be commercial markets, rather a market is a space where value is exchanged—where the need or demand is met by a supplied solution.

We may have an excellent technical solution, but if nobody wants it, there's no market. Asset managers are often concerned with asset performance, whereas other stakeholders, including the board, are concerned with company performance. From the board's perspective, value is measured in terms of the outcomes for the company as a whole, rather than for any individual asset, or group of assets. The two, however, are inextricably linked.

Just as today's temperature is tomorrow's weather report, today's asset data is tomorrow's financial statements. Are you creating value, or delivering yesterday's news?

As asset managers our role is not only to protect the value in existing assets, but also to identify sources of future value. That may be through redeploying under-utilised assets, disposing of assets that no longer deliver value, or finding non-asset solutions.

I'll go into more detail on how asset managers can take a holistic approach to value creation in Chapter 8: *Creativity*.

MASTER THE MARKET

For centuries London's watermen carried passengers both across and up and down the River Thames. The watermen rowed a small boat, called a wherry. As purchasing a wherry and a licence to operate one was very expensive, they were often handed on from father to son. A wherry was a valuable asset.

In the 18th century, horse-drawn carriages for hire started to carry people up and down the Thames, but not across it. Cabs threatened the upriver and downriver component of the watermen's trade and reduced their income.[18] Cabs were also a valuable asset, to the cab drivers, but not to the watermen.

Later in the 18th century, a major building program saw a series of new bridges span the Thames. These bridges effectively put the watermen out of business and the value of a wherry dropped considerably. Crossing the river became relatively quick and easy. The bridges were, and still are, a valuable asset to the City of London and its people.

When developing a Strategic Asset Management Plan (SAMP) it can be tempting to start with the assets. What assets do we have? How do we manage them? A waterman might have asked: How many wherries do I have? How can I improve the performance of my wherry to make it go faster? But your SAMP and your whole asset management system need to be business focused, rather than asset focused.

Key stakeholders for the watermen were their paying passengers. What did the paying passengers value? Getting from A to B safely, quickly and cheaply. They didn't want a faster wherry; they wanted a shorter journey time.

Strategy comes before assets.

There are a few watermen still on the Thames today, but the wherry is now mostly used for ceremonial purposes, not as a form of daily transport.

More recently, some of London's ageing bridges have been in need of major repairs. The Hammersmith Bridge has been closed for two years already and will require major renovations to make it fit for service again.[19] These bridges, built for horse and cart, cannot meet their intended need without careful asset management. The outage of these bridges will once again open up a temporary, if extended, need for ferry services. The value remains, not in the mode *per se*, but in crossing the river, in the safest, quickest and cheapest way possible.

As asset managers, it's critical that we understand our stakeholders, and what they value. I'm sometimes asked, 'How do we know if we've created value?' The easiest way is to ask the stakeholders themselves: what it is they value and how you'll know if you've delivered it.

Stranded asset risk

Stranded asset risk is an important consideration that has been historically under-recognised. Just as assets, like the wherry, may become technologically redundant when they're superseded by a newer model or an alternative solution, assets may also become politically or economically redundant. Even if you're the best blacksmith, you don't want to be the last blacksmith when horses make way for cars.

Stranded assets are assets that suffer from unanticipated or premature write-downs, devaluations, or conversion to liabilities. For example, coal-based assets potentially could become 'stranded' if government policies and consumer preferences force a move away from fossil fuels. This shift has been underway for some time, but many organisations, and indeed some governments, have been slow to respond.

Many car manufacturers have been ahead of the game, investing in electric vehicle technology and winding down their commitments to internal-combustion products. Because they operate in global markets, the countries that have been early adopters of bans on petrol engines have provided the commercial impetus for manufacturers to make these changes. Countries who have lagged behind in their regulatory approach will find themselves left with few options but to buy what is being built. It's safer to be proactive than to believe 'it won't happen here'.

More recently, we've seen whole new classes of assets suffer stranded asset risk as a result of the global pandemic—commercial aircraft, cruise ships, university facilities and inner-city office blocks. Reduction of travel and a wholesale shift to working from home have fundamentally changed the utilisation patterns of a wide range of assets and infrastructure. As well as climate-exposed assets, we need to identify and make provision for pandemic-exposed assets.

Senior leaders routinely assess the overall risks to their organisation in the context of the contemporary environment and predicted future trends. These risks are best weighed against the opportunities available in such an environment. When you are involved in, or advising on, these decisions it's important to understand your company's exposure to stranded asset risk and to give adequate consideration to these risks in your decision making.

The negative impacts on climate-exposed assets are fairly clear. Reduced returns on existing investment in assets of this type and long-term capital losses are likely. As well, the likelihood that an asset will become stranded may lead to reduced investment in the maintenance and upkeep of that asset. This could increase unplanned shutdowns, service interruptions and safety hazards such as explosions, crushing and falls. All of these factors are likely to further undermine the reputation of companies that own or invest in these assets and will further reduce investor confidence.

The potential for assets to become stranded is an important consideration in asset management. Climate change and the associated changes in demand for coal-based products pose a risk to companies that have coal-dependent assets. The current and future pandemics pose risks for pandemic-exposed assets. While the problem of stranded assets can be seen as negative, the emphasis on a movement away from these investments also opens up new opportunities, such as investments in remote meeting technology, renewable energy and 'Clean' or 'Green' portfolios.

To master the market, it's essential for asset managers to be informed on these issues and to be aware of their potential impacts on your organisation, not just in the long term, but also in the short to medium term. As we take a risk-based approach to asset management, the biggest risk is not that the asset will fail, but that the market will fail to need the asset.

Which of your assets are vulnerable?

MASTER YOUR MARKET

Mastery requires deliberate practice. You won't become masterful at anything by accident.

Part of this deliberate practice is ongoing personal reflection. When can you set aside time and make space to reflect on your own expectations, your ambitions, and what you need to focus on to take the next step?

Coaching and mentoring are valuable ways to make this space and time, and to provide a sounding board for your self-reflection with a trusted person who can ask pertinent questions and prompt you to consider possibilities you may have overlooked.

Part of your reflection time is understanding the market for your skills and how you ensure they remain relevant in a changing environment as you move through your career. None of us wants to become a stranded asset!

Mastering our expectations

In preparation for the 1976 Munich Olympics, the specifications for gymnastics scoreboards required three digits, including two decimal places. Officials had determined that a scoreboard that could display up to 9.99 would more than meet their needs, since a score of 10.00 was 'impossible'.

But nobody told Nadia Comaneci. When the fourteen-year-old Romanian became the first gymnast in Olympic history to score a perfect 10.00, the scoreboard displayed 1.00. She went on to score a total of seven perfect 10s during that Olympics, winning three gold medals.

The scoreboard manufacturers and the officials who commissioned them based their specifications on solid historical data and a lifetime of experience. Meanwhile, in gymnasiums around the world young people were sweating and striving every day in pursuit of that elusive score. Were they really chasing an impossible dream?

The systems we use to measure performance shouldn't limit what that performance can be. More importantly, we should define our own success and not be constrained by the limitations that others impose upon themselves. A goal isn't a limit: it's a starting point.

There's a real danger in setting the bar too low and it's important to be mindful of when others might try to do this to you. If Nadia Comaneci had believed she could never score a perfect 10, she wouldn't have done it. If she'd taken on board the limitations set by the officials, she may also never have achieved her historic feat.

In our own careers and in our roles as leaders, we need to be alert to the soft bigotry of low expectations. This is where we limit someone's options or possibilities because we make a false assumption about their abilities or ambitions. This occurs commonly, and subtly, but powerfully, for many marginalised groups, including women, people of colour, and people living with a disability.

Graeme Innes, a lawyer and Human Rights Commissioner, was blind from birth. He describes how his parents placed the 'same expectations on me as on my brother and sister'. They taught him 'to not limit someone by setting the expectations bar too low'. Instead, says Graeme, 'Life was about finding a way'.[20]

As leaders, it's critical that we don't impose these limitations on those we lead. Likewise, it's essential that we don't impose these limitations on ourselves. One of the positives about a career in asset management is that it draws on many disciplines. Regardless of your background, there are opportunities to progress by taking a mindful and deliberate approach to your own career development.

Mastering our time

I live in the subtropical city of Brisbane, in Queensland, Australia. Every spring, around early September, it's exciting to see the first jacaranda blossoms of the season. These flowers have a distinctive purple-blue hue and their vibrant colour brightens the landscape right across the city.

Jacaranda blossoms are very delicate and as they fall from the tree, they create a soft, rich carpet. The arrival of the jacarandas excites me now, but it wasn't always the case. As an undergraduate at the University of Queensland, the sight of those first blooms was always a cause for great fear and dread. It heralded the imminent arrival of exams and a very stressful time of year. It was said that if you hadn't started studying before you saw your first jacaranda flower—it was too late!

Part of the folklore at the university was that if a jacaranda blossom fell on your head, you would forget everything you'd learned. You would never see students sitting under jacaranda trees in bloom. That's a shame because they are magnificent trees, with strong branches and sweet, delicate blossoms. Since my first graduation, I now welcome the appearance of the beautiful blossoms and the upcoming festive season.

I may not have the same exam pressures as I did when I was an undergrad, but I still have deadlines. Some are externally imposed, but many are the deadlines I set for myself. Like writing my next book. Of course, I have to set time aside to do the work required to meet these deadlines and certainly at times this generates stress, as I struggle to balance commitments and get everything done.

During writing of one of my earlier books, a friend said to me, 'Don't worry, they're only self-imposed deadlines'. The implication is that deadlines we set for ourselves are somehow less important than those set by others. If we set the deadlines ourselves, then surely, we can change them to suit ourselves? I think that's only partly true. Students don't choose the date of the exam, but they do choose to study a particular course and to put themselves through a process that involves examination. In some way most deadlines are self-imposed.

If we can't keep to the deadlines we set for ourselves, how can we keep to the deadlines imposed by others, including our clients or our employer? If we want to achieve anything in life, we need to have an end-point in mind. There are many demands on our time and energy. So, why do we consider our own goals to be less important?

I challenge you today to set one goal for yourself that you'll complete before the last jacaranda blossom falls.

What will yours be?

Mastering our focus

When I was a young girl, my grandmother had a beautiful rose garden. It was formally laid out, right next to the house that sat in a clearing on a hilltop, surrounded by about five hundred acres of native forest.

My Gran tended her roses carefully. Fertilizing with manure and pruning in winter were all part of keeping the roses in full bloom. It seems counterintuitive, to cut something back in order to help it grow—but any gardener knows that a good prune is essential to healthy growth. Growth may happen anyway, but it will be slower, messier and more erratic.

Gardening guru Peter Cundall advises that 'roses are among the toughest of all plants. Even if you ignore them, they'll continue to flower, but there is no question they do benefit with a good winter prune'.

In your career, a good prune can also work wonders. We tend to accumulate commitments, saying yes when we probably shouldn't, adding to our time burden because we want to be helpful, or because we see a potential opportunity and quickly suffer from that 21st century malady of FOMO (Fear of Missing Out). A regular 'prune' of your obligations and commitments will help you focus on what's really important to you. It's easy to be busy. It's easy to generate activity, but is it progressive?

Are you growing a beautiful rose bush or a wild thicket of thorny lantana?

What will you prune, and what will you keep?

MASTER YOUR MIND

Mastery in any endeavour requires a positive approach. There's a lot to learn, and enormous effort required to pursue a desired pathway in any field. There will always be obstacles and challenges. Having confidence in your own ability to overcome these and to seek support when needed is essential to ongoing success.

Even the most talented and successful athletes need a coach. Coaching has been an integral part of my ongoing professional and personal development for many years. Three great coaches have had a significant impact on my career. They've helped me to develop presence, to build confidence, and to improve my resilience. In each case the coaching experience helped me move on to bigger and better things.

Presence

People who've met me in a business context may not realise that I'm an extreme introvert. When I first started going to corporate functions, I found them paralysing. I was terrified of talking to anyone and would wait for others to start a conversation. Even though I wanted to contribute to the conversation, I found it difficult.

Michael Doneman, of Edgeware, is a coach who helped me to overcome this fear. I met Michael when I studied Creative Industries as a postgraduate student, and I felt that there was a good alignment between our approaches. During my coaching program with Michael, I worked on my 'ferociousness' so that I could let my true self shine through, giving people I meet the opportunity to know me better.

With Michael's drama background and active meditation practice, he helped me to become more conscious of the connections between my mind and my body. I felt more comfortable in my personal and professional interactions, which helped me to take on new challenges that I may have avoided in the past.

Confidence

In 2012, I was privileged to win a scholarship to Harvard Business School, through my university's (QUT) Alumni program, Fostering Executive Women. The Harvard Women's Leadership Forum was truly transformational, and the coach assigned to each of us was a key part of this experience. Pam Lassiter, my coach for this program, is quietly spoken, definitely not the 'rah! rah!' style of coach that some people might imagine. I didn't need pushing to work harder or to achieve more, I had that covered. Instead, I needed permission to stop, to think more deeply and to reflect more fully. Pam's coaching style gave me that opportunity and I was able to make some important decisions about who I am and what I want from my career and my life.

The Harvard experience dramatically improved my confidence in many contexts. As a coach, Pam had the wisdom and insight to ask the right questions at the right moments. I was able to see that even if I work alone, I don't need to walk alone. This gave me the confidence to be secure in my decisions and to genuinely acknowledge the value I can bring to make a difference in the world. On my way home from Harvard, probably for the first time in my life, I struck up a conversation with a stranger on the train. For me this was proof that the experience had made a real difference and that I was now open to new opportunities.

Resilience

Not long after I returned from Harvard, I was pregnant with my first child. I experienced nine months of morning sickness followed by the arrival of a beautiful baby girl and then six months of complete sleep deprivation. Becoming a new parent challenged my resilience and I needed to find strategies to meet these demands.

Josie Thomson was recommended to me as an outstanding coach who would challenge my thinking. Josie is open and compassionate and, through her neuroscience insights, helped me to change some of the habits that were no longer serving me well. With Josie's guidance I improved my resilience and I now feel better able to manage the many demands of this stage of life while still maintaining my health, nurturing my relationships and growing my business.

I've never been in favour of a one-size-fits-all approach. In my own work I think it's important to apply the appropriate measures for the challenge at hand. Through each stage of my career, I've sought different coaches for the particular challenges I've faced. Great coaches have helped me to come out of my shell, to improve my confidence and to build my resilience.

Coaching, with its one-on-one delivery and individualised focus, provides a flexible addition to my overall professional and personal development program. In each case where I've sought coaching, I've been open and willing to change and ready to take certain risks to improve my outcomes. The coaches I've worked with have acknowledged this as an important part of the success of coaching. In the future I'll need different coaches for different reasons and I'll continue to seek those who are the best fit for my needs at the time.

REFERENCES

[17] Gleick, J. *The Information.* London: Harper Collins, 2011.

[18] Freedland, J., Composer. *The Long View: The rise of Uber and the plight of London's Watermen.* [Sound Recording]. British Broadcasting Corporation, 2017.

[19] London Borough of Hammersmith & Fulham, "LBHF Transport and Roads", 2021. [Online]. Available: https://www.lbhf.gov.uk/transport-and-roads/hammersmith-bridge-all-you-need-know-and-latest-updates

[20] Innes, G. *Finding a Way.* Brisbane: University of Queensland, 2016.

CHAPTER 7

TENACITY

TENACITY

ANALYSE RISKS

Indecision stifles success. When the decisions required mount up in number or complexity, it can be overwhelming, even crippling. We can only make one decision at a time, but the stream of decisions is endless. It's easy, then, to put a decision off till later, while we 'think about it a bit more'. This is quite often wise, but the choice to defer decision making on a particular matter is a decision in itself.

Deferring decision making can add to stress and anxiety, as the decisions to be made back up like a fatberg in a sewerage pipe. It may also mean that we miss out on important opportunities. As asset managers we're trained to analyse risks, but the fear of failures or catastrophic consequences can sometimes thwart our ability to seize opportunities. A keen awareness of risk should be an enabler of better decision making, rather than a deterrent.

Tenacity is an essential leadership asset that enables us to persist and carry on, even in the face of hardship and challenges. Tenacity requires that we continue to make decisions, often under difficult circumstances, when we might rather give up. Instead we need to put one foot in front of the other and as Winston Churchill is said to have urged, 'When you are going through hell, keep going'.

SURVIVAL IS EASY

Survival is our most powerful human instinct. People don't take much convincing to work for their own survival. We eat, we mate, and we protect our young. These are all part of ensuring not only our own survival, but the survival of our species.

When survival is at stake, nothing else matters. People can do extraordinary things in these situations. When Ernest Shackleton set off for Antarctica in 1914 it was billed as a grand adventure. In the days before GPS or modern thermal clothing such an adventure carried genuine risks.

When I was at Harvard Business School, we studied the case of Shackleton with Professor Nancy Koehn.[21] When their ship was lost in the ice floes, Shackleton and every one of his crew survived for eighteen months, stranded in the freezing Antarctic wilderness. They devoted their time and effort to the simple daily tasks of staying alive—cooking, eating, staying warm, and marking the passing of time. There was nothing more important.

When survival is no longer at stake, motivating people toward a common goal is hard. Not because the goal is too big, but because it's not big enough. In a quote often attributed, perhaps erroneously, to Chekov, it's said that 'Any idiot can face a crisis—it's the day to day living that wears you out!'

Tenacity requires purpose

Tenacity, then, requires purpose. To keep going in the face of inevitable challenges requires that we have a reason to get out of bed in the morning. If our survival is not at stake, what is our driver?

To persist in the long term in the face of challenges requires a belief that there's a higher purpose we're working towards—one that benefits others besides ourselves. Dr Angela Duckworth, bestselling author of *Grit*, studied sixteen thousand American adults and found a clear relationship between 'purpose' and 'grit'. The most tenacious people were those who believed that 'My work makes the world a better place'.[22]

This sense of purpose extends beyond the transactional nature of a job—being a necessity to fulfil the basic needs of life—and even beyond a career, where one job may be seen as a stepping-stone to another. Instead, those with high levels of purpose and grit saw their work as a calling. There isn't a single type of job that fulfils the criteria of a calling. Rather, it's your own perspective that defines what your purpose is and how your work contributes to that purpose.

Grit begets grit

Are gritty people more successful, or are successful people more gritty?

It's a classic chicken-and-egg conundrum. While we know they are related, which came first?

Dr Duckworth explains that it's most likely both. Her work included studying the relationship between commitment to extracurricular activities in one's youth and success later in life. She writes that 'following through on our commitments while we grow up both requires grit and, at the same time, builds it'.[22]

It's similar to building strength through weight training. While it takes strength to lift weights, the more you do it, the stronger you'll get.

Tenacity is one of the important assets leaders need to carry on in the face of prolonged uncertainty and constant change. When your role involves managing risks, for yourselves and for others, and when you're responsible for the performance and wellbeing of your team, tenacity keeps you hanging in there.

What are you doing to build your grit muscle?

Tenacity requires hope

My Dad always said, 'The harder I work, the luckier I get'. We know that success is not a matter of luck, but the tenacity required for success does require a measure of hope. Without a belief that there's a positive future ahead of the present challenge, it's easy to give up. Lack of hope becomes a self-fulfilling prophecy. If we don't believe that we can, then of course, we can't.

We need to believe that our own efforts can in some way progress us towards that positive future, even if there are external factors beyond our control. For Shackleton and his crew, hope was essential. In the inhospitable Antarctic landscape, without the benefit of modern communications, it would have been easy to lose hope that they'd ever get back home to the other side of the world. It would have been easy to assume that they'd been left for dead, frozen forever in an icy grave.

Instead, they chose to hope. Led by Shackleton they maintained routines, played music and celebrated Christmas and birthdays. They acted as though life would go on, and it did—one day at a time.[21]

NO RISK DOESN'T EXIST

Some years ago, as a board director, I was involved in negotiations with another company for a potential joint venture. Part of my role was to identify and assess the strategic risks to our company. At one point in the conversation, the CEO of the other company made the statement that 'There is no risk'.

Far from reassuring me, this statement undermined the credibility of this CEO. How could they really believe that there was no risk? No risk doesn't exist.

Assessing risks takes judgement because it's not absolute. Those threats that are 'rare' don't usually draw a lot of interest, unless the consequence is catastrophic, in which case they are noted, but in practice largely dismissed as 'impossible'.

During the global pandemic, we saw what catastrophic can really look like. We've had to re-set our perception of risk and redefine 'impossible'. As we re-set our risk thermostat, we might question our judgement. After all, how can we know for sure?

The reality is we can never know for sure where and when threats may arise. But we can be sure of one thing: no risk doesn't exist.

How are you re-setting your risk thermostat?

Tenacity requires analysing risks

Nobody wants to think about risk when things are going well, but it only takes a moment for things to turn from very good to horrid.

Asset management takes a risk-based approach to creating value from assets. One of the fundamental questions is 'What could go wrong?' Risk is a key focus for board directors and can be a good starting point when opening a conversation with the board on asset management.

Asset managers typically have a focus on operational risks and use techniques such as FMECA (failure mode, effects and criticality analysis) to identify what could go wrong, what the impact could be, and how that impact could be avoided or mitigated. In other words, what will happen if this asset fails? What will the consequences be? How much will it cost?

While operational risks are important, as you progress through your career, you will need to develop the capability to look beyond these operational risks to the full range of strategic risks faced by your organisation. These include operational risks and financial risks, but also extend to environmental risks, reputational risks and political risks.

For example, asset obsolescence is an important factor in investment decisions and the risk of carrying stranded assets is a significant strategic consideration. Just as assets may become technologically redundant when they are replaced with a newer model, assets may also become politically or economically redundant. Strategically, the more important question is not 'Will the asset fail?' but 'Will the market fail to need the asset anymore?'

A fundamental characteristic of risk is that it relates to the unknown. In 2014, Sony Pictures Entertainment was hit by a disabling cyber-attack that brought the company to a standstill. This was a known risk, against which they were unprotected. Their executive director of information security at the time said, 'I won't invest $10 million to avoid a possible $1 million loss. It's a valid business decision to accept the risk'. However, this turned out to be a gross underestimate. The direct costs of the attack were over $100 million, not including the reputational costs and flow-on impacts to individual staff whose personal information was stolen.[23]

As an asset manager your role in risk is to reduce the unknowns by raising both your own awareness and the awareness of others. You will need to ask questions like:

How well are we balancing risk against cost and performance?

Are our information systems adequately supporting a risk-based approach?

Are our valuable intangible assets as well protected as our valuable tangible assets?

Have I locked the car, or did I leave the keys in the ignition?

Regardless of the type of risk being considered, the fundamental questions remain the same: what could go wrong, and how can we prevent it?

You can develop the tenacity required to move from the workshop to the boardroom by analysing risks over time and across contexts. The same technical skills you've gained to analyse operational risks can be applied to analyse other types of risks as you take on higher level roles.

Risk is relative

When we're analysing risks, it's important to remember that risk is always relative. In a radio interview I heard with Mark Webber, Australian Formula One racing driver, he said, 'We risk everything. We risk the car. We risk ourselves. We risk everything to get to the front of the grid'. This is very different to a commercial airline that treats passenger safety as its highest priority and can't tolerate a mechanical failure in mid-air. The risk appetite is different, the measure of performance is different, and the importance of cost is also relative. The risks that are acceptable in your context will change over time and between different roles that you may work in. Acceptable risk depends on both risk appetite and risk capacity, which varies between organisations and between individuals within the organisation.

Risk and return

Risk and return are inherently linked. We know that an established 'blue chip' stock will give solid returns more consistently than a new start-up. Investors choose these 'safer' stocks not for their spectacular returns, but for their reliable income. This is popular with retirees or those coming close to retirement who need to live off their savings and investments. On the other hand, start-ups are more speculative and carry greater risk. The company is unknown and untested, and it might fail. However, if it succeeds, the few dollars you invest now have the potential for huge returns. In the finance world, that return is the pay-off for the risk you take.

Twenty years ago, I took my first trip to Germany and visited the Deutsche Boerse, the German Stock Exchange, in Frankfurt. These were the days before the euro currency was introduced and they still traded in Deutsche marks. Outside the Exchange, on the Boersenplatz are two bronze statues: a bull and a bear. They represent the rising and the falling market respectively.

Twelve years later when I was in New York, I took a tour of the financial district with a guide who was a former Wall Street banker. As in Frankfurt, there's a bronze statue of a bull on a traffic island near the New York Stock Exchange. I asked my guide the obvious question: 'Where's the bear?'

'Bear?' he scoffed. 'There's no bear on Wall Street'.

It might seem foolish, but optimism is inherently human. It's what gets us out of bed in the morning. It's what keeps us going when things get tough. On the Boersenplatz, the bull and the bear are locked in an eternal tussle. When the bull rears, the bear ducks. When the bear growls, the bull keeps fighting. There is no winner in their struggle. When we hear the bear growl, the important question is not, 'Who will win?' but 'How will we rise to the challenge?'

Business risks are as important as technical risks

To create value, the value gained needs to exceed the risks taken. Analysing business risks is critical.

RESILIENCE EQUALS SELF-CARE

So, a military force has no constant formation, water has no constant shape; the ability to gain victory by changing and adapting according to the opponent is called genius.

Sun-Tzu[24]

When I was studying for a PhD in Strategy, Sun Tzu was compulsory reading. In the twenty years since then, I've continued to revisit these ancient writings each year, always gleaning something new.

The military metaphor has been widely used in business. It encourages us to think of our business competitors as our enemies and our goal as defeating them. While knowing our competitive environment is essential, one of the main limitations of the military metaphor is that it assumes a 'zero sum game'. In other words, there is one winner and one loser—victory must be gained at all costs.

The other limitation is that this 'win at all costs' mentality can lead us into stressful, unhealthy lives where we ignore the very things that give us the strength we need to compete. The essence of Sun Tzu's *The Art of War* draws on Chinese Taoist philosophies that see the 'peak efficiency of knowledge and strategy is to make conflict altogether unnecessary: to overcome others' armies without fighting is the best of skills'.[24]

Leaders who practise timely retreat, individually and with their teams, return refreshed. Their competitors who have struggled on—unwilling to rest—are tired, hungry and battle weary.

For Shackleton's crew, one of the keys to their survival was the resilience of their leader. Every day, he had to 'show up'. If he didn't look after himself, he would have been no use to any of them.

To nurture the tenacity we need to take a leading role in our own career, we must nurture our own self-care. Building routines that allow space and time to refresh and recharge are important. It's easy to get carried away with a focus on work, but family, friends and leisure pursuits are also important for our development as a leader.

Time out doesn't need to be a day spa, or Zen meditation, although these are both excellent! Personally, I enjoy a float tank, to literally take the weight off my shoulders. Any activity that takes your mind off work stresses is time well spent—cooking, fishing, cycling, gardening, music, sport or arts and crafts are all ways we can rest our brains and maintain our tenacity.

As well as analysing technical and business risks, tenacity requires that we analyse risks to our own health. Be proactive about your health and wellbeing and seek professional advice when you need it. Just as we use preventative maintenance to ensure the longevity of the assets we manage, we need to practise preventative health to minimise risks and ensure peak performance throughout our careers.

How are you taking care of yourself?

REFERENCES

[21] Koehn, N. et al. *Leadership in Crisis: Ernest Shackleton and the Epic Voyage of the Endurance.* 2003 (Revised 2010). Harvard Business School Case 803-127.

[22] Duckworth, A. *Grit: Why passion and resilience are the secrets to success.* London: Vermilion, 2017.

[23] Elkind, P. "Sony Picture: Inside the Hack of the Century", *Fortune,* no. July 2015.

[24] Sun-Tzu. *The Art of War.* T. Cleary, Ed., Boston: Shambhala Dragon Editions, 1988 Translation.

CHAPTER 8

CREATIVITY

CREATIVITY

CREATE VALUE

Destruction makes headlines—and breaks hearts. In recent years the term 'doom-scrolling' has come to describe the activity of scrolling through a news feed of destructive headlines, a habit that can lead to anxiety, depression and a general feeling of impending doom.

Fires, floods, pandemics, recessions all wreak their own destruction, and can follow each other in quick succession, with no apparent relief. With destruction all around us, it can be hard to feel that's there's any room for growth.

The counter to destruction is creation. Creativity is innately human, but it's easy for people in technical roles to feel that creativity plays no part in their work—and even to believe that they are 'not creative'. Creating value for stakeholders through assets is the core purpose of asset management. So it's essential for asset managers to be creative. But creating value is not as simple as it sounds.

Traditionally, value creation in asset management is seen through the lenses of cost, risk and performance. Using this perspective, value can be created by reducing costs, by reducing risks and by improving performance. This is a good starting point, but it can underplay the multi-faceted, and inherently subjective, nature of value.

In practice, asset management is often focused more on protecting existing value than on identifying new sources of value. Similarly, there is an important focus on delivering value to stakeholders through the services assets enable, but often less emphasis on demonstrating the value of asset management itself. For the discipline of asset management to remain relevant in a rapidly changing world, we need to take a holistic approach to value creation, and to ensure that as asset management professionals we are skilled in both identifying value and demonstrating that value.

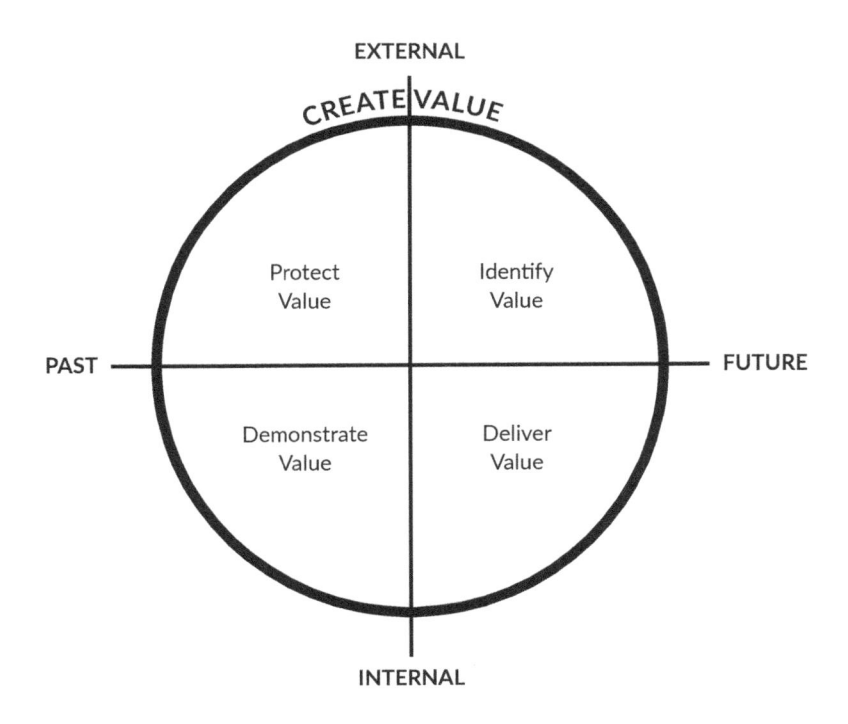

Figure 3: A holistic model for value creation

PROTECT VALUE

If we start with what we already own, stemming erosion of value by protecting existing assets is an essential part of the risk-based approach of asset management. Traditional methodologies, such as FMECA, ask us to consider 'What could go wrong?' However, protecting what we already have, while important, doesn't on its own create new value. A focus solely on protecting existing value without identifying new sources of value can create exposure to stranded asset risk.

Stranded asset risk has historically been under-emphasised. A growing awareness of climate change risks has lifted the focus on this issue, particularly in regard to fossil fuel-related assets, but the global pandemic has led to diverse types of assets, including aircraft, cruise ships, university facilities and commercial office buildings, being subject to stranded asset risk.

We need to take value creation beyond the traditional, fixed approach of reducing cost, reducing risk and improving performance. The corollary of each of these provides us instead with a growth approach.

Value can be created not only by reducing costs, but also by increasing revenue. Reducing risk is essential, but so is identifying and exploiting opportunities. Likewise, improving performance is not just about doing something better; it's also about removing the constraints that can limit the achievable level of performance.

Where stranded asset or passive asset risks exist, redeploying underutilised assets, or employing existing resources for a novel use are ways to create value by focusing on increased revenue, enhanced opportunities and removal of constraints.

	Fixed approach	Growth approach
	↓ Cost	↑ Revenue
	↓ Risk	↑ Opportunities
	↑ Performance	↓ Constraints

Table 4: A fixed versus growth approach

Identify value

In his research, Kent Miller outlines three ways that we can identify opportunities to create value:[25]

1. Recognise opportunity
2. Discover opportunity
3. Create opportunity.

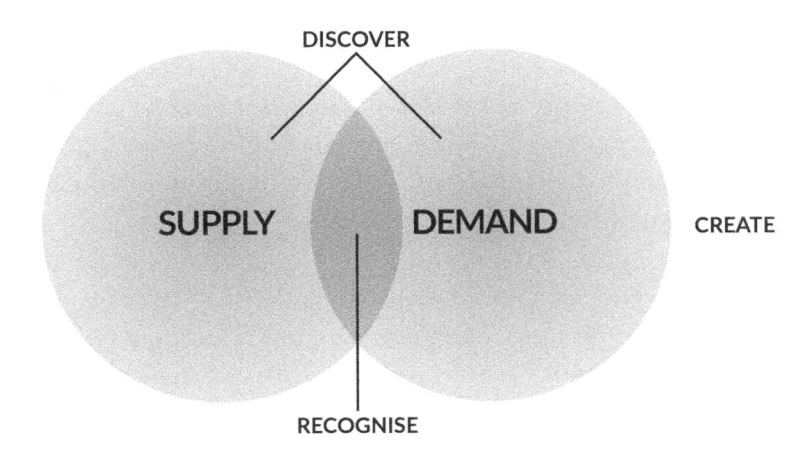

Figure 4: Three ways to identify opportunities

CHAPTER 8: CREATIVITY   125

Firstly, to recognise opportunity we need to match sources of supply and demand that already exist. This is like a real estate agent who matches the seller of a property with a buyer for the property. The negotiated transaction creates value for the buyer, for the seller and for the agent.

Secondly, we can discover opportunity when either demand or supply exist, but not both. We have seen this as the pressing global imperative for a coronavirus vaccine has driven international collaboration between scientists to create a solution. This is the case whenever a pharmaceutical company creates a drug that will treat an illness for which there is no existing treatment. Latent demand from the sufferers of the illness is met by the creation of a solution that meets their needs. Value is created for the patient, for the pharmaceutical company, for the community and for various other participants in the supply chain.

Thirdly, we can create opportunity when neither supply nor demand already exist, a concept earlier described by Sarasvathy et al.[26] The smart phone is a great example of creating opportunity. There was no existing demand for a device that had not yet been created. We didn't know we needed it until it existed. Both the supply and the demand needed to be developed, a process that required creativity and innovative thinking.

Value is created in exchange and is always relative. What one person values, another does not—one person's trash is another's treasure. Value delivery is often focused on the processes that enable that delivery. This is essential, but while processes deliver outputs, people deliver outcomes. The value is in the outcome achieved for the stakeholders involved in the value exchange. In this sense, the outcome is more important than the process itself.

Deliver value

To effectively deliver value and a desired outcome, established processes may need to be changed, adapted, or even abandoned. Again, we've seen this in the development process for COVID-19 vaccines. The impetus was strong for scientists around the world to collaborate, rather than to corral their research as they would customarily do. Prestigious journals such as the *New England Journal of Medicine* have published research in as little as 48 hours, a process that would usually take several years. The traditional drawn-out research and regulatory processes have been sped up dramatically because the need for a timely outcome was greater than the potential risk of using a new, and previously untested, process.[27]

Demonstrate value

Demonstrating value could be seen simply as a compliance obligation. Mandatory reporting of various types exists in every industry. However, using data and other tools to demonstrate value can, in turn, open opportunities for further value creation. Demonstrating the value of a certain practice or initiative provides evidence to support further investment or allocation of resources in that area.

To create value, a delivered service must have meaning and relevance. A company's innovation ethos is linked to its growth trajectory.[28] A company with an owner-ethos focuses on tangible capital assets and relies on passive capital growth for their returns. In the current environment, this capital growth is often negative, and many owners face stranded asset risk.

By contrast, ideas as assets, which are purely intangible, provide the potential for unconstrained growth. This fits with a creator ethos, which recognises that ideas, not just objects, have value. Theoretically, there is no limit on the number of times an idea can be sold. Creation of the idea itself requires relatively small capital investment. The required risk capacity is low and the potential return on investment is high.[28]

IDEAS ARE OUR MOST IMPORTANT ASSETS

The imperative for innovation has dominated the first part of the 21st century. Economic, technological and environmental drivers have seen the pace of change outstrip the capability of many companies and some industries to adapt. A global pandemic has brought these imperatives into stark relief. In the face of immense human challenges, a creative approach is more important than ever. The pandemic has also changed our perception of risk. As a risk-based discipline, asset management has a critical role to play in re-calibrating for the future and contributing to economic and social recovery in the years and decades ahead.

It may be counterintuitive to think that we can initiate innovation in the path of catastrophe, but the silt left by flood waters creates a rich and fertile environment to nourish fresh, green shoots. When looking to re-start growth after a catastrophic shock, ideas are our most essential assets.

Before the industrial revolution, wealth was based on owning land. With each subsequent wave of technological innovation, potential for growth has been further separated from the ownership of tangible assets. According to research by Ocean Tomo, the impact of the coronavirus has accelerated the existing trend towards an increasing proportion of total assets of major companies being intangible, rather than tangible. In 2020, it's estimated that 90% of total market value of companies in the S&P 500 is held in intangible assets. This trend holds for the S&P Europe 350 which reached 74% of market value in intangible assets as of 2020.[29]

COMPONENTS OF S&P 500 MARKET VALUE

Year	Tangible Assets	Intangible Assets
1975	17%	83%
1985	32%	68%
1995	68%	32%
2005	80%	20%
2015	84%	16%
2020	90%	10%

Figure 5: Components of S&P 500 Market Value 2020 [29]

A company that uses its property assets to generate value through traditional leasing arrangements may experience a decline in growth, as commercial customers move away from the desire for long-term property holdings and prefer more flexible use of space. This development has been enabled by the uptake of technologies that see more people working away from a traditional office environment. With the rapid rise of working from home, companies around the globe are reducing their office footprint. An owner of commercial property could innovate their business model by moving away from traditional leasing arrangements to offer 'space as a service' with more flexible access to space through weekly, daily or even hourly hiring that better meets the needs of their customers. An example is the company Liquid Space.[30]

This is also apparent is in the automotive industry. Countries across the world are legislating to ban production of new internal combustion engines on a staggered timeline[31] that includes:

- Norway 2025
- India 2030
- China 2030
- Netherlands 2030
- Germany 2030
- France 2040
- Britain 2040.

Given this timeline, the market for new traditional vehicles will be all but gone within 10 years from now. Car manufacturers who operate in a global market are already shifting their investment in plant and technology to meet this shift. Even if a country such as Australia hasn't introduced similar legislation, they will have no choice but to adopt the products produced for the global markets. This also has implications for component and accessory manufacturers, such as those for spark plugs.

Asset management has grown from a traditional base around physical, tangible assets. A focus on protecting what we own from known and foreseeable risks is a core part of that work. A recognition of the importance of intangible assets expands the scope of asset management and ensures that these principles and our skills remain relevant and highly valued. Creative ideas provide the next step that will set us on our path for future growth. For a resilient future, what we create is more important than what we own.

IDEAS DON'T COME OUT OF NOWHERE

In the chapter on *Ingenuity*, I spoke about the myth of the hero scientist—Newton being struck by an apple, Archimedes leaping from the bath exclaiming 'Eureka!' Our attachment to this myth can lead us to believe that innovation requires a lightning bolt of genius inspiration.

But what if inspiration never strikes?

This belief can feed a fear of failure and the perception that innovation is based on random chance and therefore perceived as high risk. In reality, lightning bolts don't come out of the blue. The storm has to brew first. On a summer afternoon the humidity builds, the sky darkens, rumbles echo in the distance, until the moment is right for the storm to break. Fear of failure can hold us back, but we have no need to be intimidated by these hero stories. Instead, we can harness our inherent human creativity and nurture an environment in which it can flourish.

When I was a postgraduate student, I had the great privilege to spend some time in the University of Queensland's Fryer Library to examine Peter Carey's original manuscripts for the novel *Oscar and Lucinda*. The purpose of my research was to study the author's writing practice. Through six boxes of archived materials, I was able to observe patterns in the writer's daily habits and his approach to creating a major new work from the kernel of an idea to the finished novel.

Peter Carey's practice is to sit down to his typewriter at 9.00 am each day and to write at least 4 pages. Some days it would be many more. Many ideas would be captured in initial notes, but only some would be further developed and end up as part of the final work. Ideas, plot threads, even character names and the name of the story itself could change many times during the development of the novel.

Even if your work is not about writing novels, you can learn from Peter Carey that creative work requires daily practice. Professional creative artists don't sit around waiting for inspiration. They schedule time to explore and develop ideas as part of their everyday work. For innovation to be effective, working with new ideas needs to be part of daily practice, not a sporadic or ad hoc activity.

We can schedule innovation the way we schedule maintenance. Allowing time for creative thought and idea generation is essential to any kind of intellectual work. It's important for each of us to make time and space for our own creative thinking. As leaders it's also important for us to provide our teams with time and space dedicated to essential thinking—both so that individuals have that space and so that the team has time together.

IDEAS ON THEIR OWN ARE NOT INNOVATION

Just as a raw steak on a plate isn't a meal, ideas on their own are not innovation. Innovation creates value from ideas, and this only happens when the ideas are implemented. An idea without implementation is just a thought bubble.

IDEA → IMPLEMENTATION → IMPACT

Figure 6: Idea to impact

Successful innovation requires commitment, consistency and collaboration. Of these, collaboration has been under most threat in recent times. Through 2020, what we historically trusted as 'safe' has changed and has influenced the way we collaborate. In 2020 scientists around the world collaborated at an escalating scale and pace. The imperative to quickly share information set aside the traditional paths to publishing scientific research findings.

For collaboration to be purposeful, it requires a conscious decision and deliberate effort to bring together people who might only usually pass in the hall. There needs to be a visible commitment to empower innovation: commitment of funds and allocation of time for innovation activities. It also means adopting a consistent approach to innovate every day, rather than one-off or occasional activities. Ad hoc innovation leads to ad hoc results.

As leaders we have a critical role in being proactive, rather than reactive, when it comes to innovation and creativity. We're not waiting for ideas to strike! Instead, we can take active steps to nurture an environment where ideas not only flourish, but are captured, analysed and effectively implemented.

This can be as simple as scheduling a weekly time for your team to meet solely for the purposes of idea sharing—not your typical 'team meeting', but an opportunity to listen, share challenges and explore new ideas.

When I worked with an architectural firm on their innovation strategy, they implemented this idea by setting aside a regular time, for just half an hour each week. The time was informal, gathered around a table with a spread of cheese and crackers. They were initially concerned that they might 'run out of things to talk about' and weren't sure if they should set a formal agenda instead. I encouraged them to go ahead with these regular collaborative moments and to keep to the schedule regardless of whether there was anything specific to discuss.

The outcome of this consistent approach has been increased connection between colleagues within the team, an enhanced sense of meaning in their work, and improved engagement with clients of the firm. A number of significant new product and service innovations have progressed from idea to impact within a 12-month period. Creating this regular time and space for connection and collaboration had benefits well beyond what they may have previously done in that 30 minutes.

Thinking time is not wasted time.

In 2020, the world changed. We faced enormous challenges, which present us now with amazing opportunities. As we take our next steps, we can choose what we carry with us, and what we leave behind. Beyond 2020, innovation is not a luxury—it's an imperative. Tangible and intangible have been transformed, and our perception of what is safe has been altered, perhaps forever.

Beyond 2020, what we create matters more than what we own. Success in our new era requires us to move beyond an individualistic focus on our own survival to embrace a collaborative approach to innovation that we embed through consistency and commitment.[32]

It's the time to focus not on what we've lost, but on what we can now create—together.

REFERENCES

[25] Miller, K. "Risk and Rationality in Entrepreneurial Processes", *Strategic Entrepreneurship Journal*, vol. 1, pp. 57-74, 2007.

[26] Sarasvathy, S., Dew, N., Velamuir, S. and Venkataraman, S. "Three Views of Entrepreneurial Opportunity", in *Handbook of Entrepreneurship Research*, S. &. A. D. Acs, Ed., Boston, Springer, 2003, pp. 141-160.

[27] Beedles, M. "Chapter 2: Begin", in *What the hell do we do now? An enterprise guide to COVID-19 and beyond*. M. Butler, A. Hagan and B. Hodgson, Eds., Melbourne, Kienco Pty Ltd, 2020, pp. 51-64.

[28] Beedles, M. "The imperative for innovation in asset management", Fremantle, 2019.

[29] Tomo, O. "Annual Study of Intangible Asset Market Value", Ocean Tomo LLC, 2020.

[30] Beedles, M. *Asset Management for Directors*. Sydney: Australian Institute of Company Directors, 2016.

[31] Fortuna, W. "The growing list of countries vowing to ban the sale of gas powered cars", Quartz, 17 October 2017. [Online].

[32] Beedles, M. "Beyond 2020: Sustaining the future of asset management", in AMPEAK, Melbourne, 2021.

STREET SMARTS

CHAPTER 9

HUMILITY

HUMILITY

IDENTIFY PRIORITIES

History is littered with disasters borne of arrogance. From *Titanic* to *Challenger*, decisions made without the humility to ask important questions have had devastating outcomes.

> *I could not imagine any condition which would cause a ship to founder. Modern shipbuilding has gone beyond that.*[33]
>
> Edward Smith, Captain of the RMS Titanic, five years before its fateful voyage.

Allan McDonald, Director of the Space Shuttle Solid Rocket Motor Project for the engineering contractor Morton Thiokol, was concerned that below-freezing temperatures might impact the integrity of the solid rockets' O-rings on the *Challenger* shuttle. The night before the shuttle was due to launch, he had refused to sign the launch recommendation over safety concerns.[34]

NASA administrators ignored McDonald's advice and the launch went ahead anyway. Later, when he shared his experiences with the shuttle program McDonald emphasised that the most important lessons were those about communication.

> *In my career, I don't know how many times people have raised their hand and said, 'This may be a dumb question, but...' I always*

> *stood up and said, 'In my entire career I've never, ever heard a dumb question. I've heard a lot of dumb answers'.*

McDonald later reflected that in his career following the disaster…

> *I decided that what's better than thinking about what could have been, and should have been, is to make sure it never happens again.*[34]

As we discussed in Chapter 5, the status quo doesn't shift just because you're right. McDonald's technical advice was sound, but he failed to influence the decision makers. He could have lived his life with an attitude of 'I told you so!' Instead, he chose to learn from the experience and by sharing these learnings, did his best to ensure that subsequent generations could tell a different story.

INFLUENCE IS ABOUT THEIR PRIORITIES, NOT YOURS

Engaging stakeholders to take an interest in your proposal or to heed your advice requires a level of influence. To be motivated to take an interest requires that the person understands how it fits with their own priorities. They're sure to ask, 'What's in it for me?' Whether it's washing hands or investing in infrastructure, human beings make decisions based on their own priorities, as they perceive them.

Engaging stakeholders requires building the three cases we've discussed in this book: the technical case, the business case and the human case. In the technical case, you are applying innovation to create solutions. In the business case, you are demonstrating impact by creating value, and in the human case, you are using influence to create meaning.

Logic is not enough to persuade people, as human decision making is not entirely rational. Aristotle's great treatise on Rhetoric, written around 350 BCE,[35] provides the underpinnings of persuasion that are still relevant today.

> *Of the modes of persuasion furnished by the spoken word there are three kinds. The first kind depends on the personal character of the speaker; the second on putting the audience into a certain frame of mind; the third on the proof, or apparent proof, provided by the words of the speech itself. Persuasion is achieved by the speaker's personal character when the speech is so spoken as to make us think him credible. We believe good men more fully and more readily than others: this is true generally whatever the question is, and absolutely true where exact certainty is impossible and opinions are divided. This kind of persuasion, like the others, should be achieved by what the speaker says, not by what people think of his character before he begins to speak. It is not true, as some writers assume in their treatises on rhetoric, that the personal goodness revealed by the speaker contributes nothing to his power of persuasion; on the contrary, his character may almost be called the most effective means of persuasion he possesses.*
>
> *Secondly, persuasion may come through the hearers, when the speech stirs their emotions. Our judgements when we are pleased and friendly are not the same as when we are pained and hostile. It is towards producing these effects, as we maintain, that present-day writers on rhetoric direct the whole of their efforts. This subject shall be treated in detail when we come to speak of the emotions.*
>
> *Thirdly, persuasion is effected through the speech itself when we have proved a truth or an apparent truth by means of the persuasive arguments suitable to the case in question.*

There are, then, these three means of effecting persuasion. The man who is to be in command of them must, it is clear, be able (1) to reason logically, (2) to understand human character and goodness in their various forms, and (3) to understand the emotions—that is, to name them and describe them, to know their causes and the way in which they are excited.[35]

Aristotle's Rhetoric is usually summarised into its three key components, as Ethos (the credibility of the speaker), Logos (logic and truth) and Pathos (the power of emotions). All three are needed to be persuasive.

Logic or facts alone are not enough to influence decision makers. This is particularly true when dealing with a highly technical subject matter where you are a specialist in your field. It's likely that many decision makers don't have your level of understanding of the subject matter. What's needed is to respect that the decision maker is an expert in their own domain and to take an approach that engages and enlightens them.

Creating the human case requires analysing priorities. Their priorities, not yours. It takes humility to put yourself in someone else's shoes, to listen carefully to your audience and to understand their concerns.

The greater the complexity, the smaller the audience

Once when travelling in Thailand I took an overnight trip from Bangkok to Kanchanaburi to visit the famous 'Bridge on the River Kwai'. I was keen to take the train over the bridge and went to the ticket office of the small railway station to purchase my fare.

As I approached the counter, I greeted the ticket seller with the traditional Thai greeting 'Sawasdee kha'. His eyes lit up and he wore a huge smile as he exclaimed with great surprise, in English, 'You speak Thai!'

Sadly, this simple greeting was the limit of my Thai language skills and thankfully, the ticket seller had very good English. The small effort I had made to greet him in his own language meant that this gentleman went out of his way to help me feel welcome and enjoy my visit to his home-town.

So often, complexity is worn as a badge of honour, but the greater the complexity, the smaller the audience. Complex, technical language is OK when you're talking with other specialists in your own field, because you're all native speakers. If you want to get your message to a wider audience, you need to speak their language.

The ticket seller understood that most of his customers were foreign tourists who wouldn't speak Thai. So, he had made an effort to learn enough of the languages his customers spoke. Starting from a perspective of respect and empathy helps to create warm connections that allow the conversation to continue, in any language.

Who is your audience and what language do they speak?

As you move through your career, the value you create will take a different form; what's required to deliver value will change. While in the early stages, you are valued most for what you do, with an emphasis on completing tasks, at the advisor stage you'll be valued for what you know and the advice you provide, based on a recognised body of knowledge that you have learned. In the advocate stage, what you think, given your experience in the field, will be valued as you add to the body of knowledge with new thinking.

At the ambassador level, when you take on very senior roles, you will be valued most for your ability to influence. Rather than just 'what you know', value will come from 'who you know' and 'who knows you'. Your personal and professional reputation becomes paramount, but humility is essential.

BUILDING CONFIDENCE, WITHOUT ARROGANCE

Humans are social creatures and not only our survival, but also our success depends on our ability to interact in a social world. While as professionals, it's important to develop confidence in our own abilities in order to do our jobs well, it's equally important to respect the professionalism of others and to apply our knowledge and expertise without arrogance or disrespect.

Recent anthropological research by the University of Oxford has identified seven cooperative behaviours that are common across more than 60 cultures studied. Rather than there being differences between cultures, cooperation was universally viewed as morally good.[36]

The seven behaviours are:

- Family values – prioritising allocation of resources to kin
- Group loyalty – co-ordinating to mutual advantage
- Reciprocity – social exchange (you scratch my back and I'll scratch yours)

- Bravery – called for in conflicts over disputed resources
- Respect – deference to elders or superiors
- Fairness – dividing disputed resources equally
- Property rights – recognising prior possession.

These are the 'rules of the game' in human societies. Of these, bravery and respect go hand in hand as part of resolving conflict. The age-old battle between the Hawk and the Dove, as immortalised in the DC Comics superheroes of the same names, shows that a defender of the group will be honoured, but so will someone who respects others and defers to their individual needs to the greater good.

A global pandemic has spurred a shift in societal focus from the individual to the collective. We've raised our level of consciousness about how even the smallest of our actions may affect others, both individually and collectively. Building confidence without arrogance also means recognising and acknowledging that our successes are not ours alone. Rather, we are supported by the collective group to achieve our own ambitions.

The myth of talent

When I was at Harvard Business School, one of the most intriguing and powerful lessons was from Boris Groysberg, who shared his research on high performing 'stars' in merchant banks on Wall Street. This research is published in his book, *Chasing Stars: The myth of talent and the portability of performance*.[37] High performers on Wall Street would be frequently poached by other banks who believed that hiring these 'stars' would improve their own company's performance. Financial analysts, just like asset managers, are in a highly technical domain, where their technical skills are necessary, but not sufficient, for success.

One of the key findings of this research is that when those so-called 'stars' moved to a new employer, their performance dropped significantly, and the promise of these high performers wasn't realised. Delving deeper into the findings revealed an exception in this highly male dominated sector. A small number of high performing women who moved companies didn't suffer the same drop in performance after the move.

Interviews with these women revealed that as minorities and cultural outsiders in the environment of Wall Street firms, they had not benefited from the internal networks within their firms that many men relied on. Instead, they had achieved their success by cultivating relationships outside the firm, focusing on building networks with customers and companies within the industries they served. When they made the move to a new firm, these external networks remained. By contrast, those who had built their success primarily on their internal networks lost these when they moved and had to start again from scratch.

Regardless of your gender or other demographic fit, the lessons learned from this research are valuable to everyone. It's never too early to build your networks. Be actively involved in your professional bodies, participate in industry forums and collective learning opportunities. Present your work at conferences and nurture relationships with suppliers and colleagues both inside and outside your own organisation. Knowing that you have established external networks will make it easier to move from one job to another, with the confidence that you can maintain your established level of performance.

THE HUMILITY TO SEEK SUPPORT

Groysberg cites, 'the most conspicuous difference between star and non-star women in equity research is access to a supportive mentor'.

According to the seminal work of Kathy Kram, mentors fulfil two main roles in enhancing the career and personal development of their protégés. Firstly, they provide career related support in the form of coaching, protection, exposure and sponsorship. Secondly, they provide psychosocial support in the form of acceptance, confirmation, counselling and friendship.[38]

An individual mentor may provide one or both of these functions. Some of these functions are best served by someone within the organisation, in terms of building internal networks. However, some are better served by those outside the company you work in, especially when it comes to the personal aspects of navigating your own path. Sometimes it's easier to share your concerns with someone who doesn't directly influence your promotional prospects.

A third role of a mentor, which has sometimes been included as one or other of the above two roles, is that of a role model. The distinction is that a role model can be someone you observe and admire, but don't know personally. It's someone whose path you seek to emulate, but with whom you may not ever have any direct contact. Many of us are influenced by such role models in our early lives and, indeed, they may be a determining factor in the career paths we choose.

Mentors we know and work with can also serve as role models. The advantage of a direct relationship is that you have the opportunity to ask them about the challenges they've faced and what it was really like to deal with certain situations. An effective mentor will be frank and open, without breaching their own obligations to the confidentiality of others. You can delve into the nitty-gritty and learn more than you might from the biography of an eminent, but distant, role model.

In the initial stages with a new company, you may find an internal mentor who can guide you on the 'way things are done around here' and will help you to adapt and understand the internal culture quickly and relatively easily. Nurturing ongoing relationships is harder if you move to another company, but external mentors can be a consistent source of support through career changes.

It's never too early to seek a mentor. Having multiple mentors, both inside and outside your organisation, to support you in the different aspects of your career development will help you to realise your own leadership potential. Approaching a mentoring relationship with the humility of a learner can bring great benefits. Mentors can help to demystify the next steps and give you the confidence to extend your ambitions.

Practising humility

Humility is ultimately about respect for others. This means taking the time and giving the attention to listen deeply and to connect on a human level. When I was in my mid-twenties, I quite suddenly and permanently lost the hearing in my left ear. I'd had a cold for a few weeks and doctors suspect that the neurological damage to my inner ear was caused by this virus.

It came as a shock, and due to the nature of the damage, a hearing aid doesn't really help. I had to learn to adapt to a changed way of interacting with people in order to be able to communicate, which was very frustrating and stressful at first. It required me to stop and to listen carefully, to give my full attention to the person speaking, to face them and to make deliberate eye contact. It required me to focus on listening, not just hearing.

Oscar Trimboli, in his book *Deep Listening: Impact beyond words*, describes five levels of listening that go beyond the technical activity of hearing the words being spoken.[39]

Firstly, listening to **yourself**, to identify the barrier to your own ability to listen well and to clear your mind of the clutter that might interfere.

Secondly, listening to the **content**, the words themselves, which are important, but are not the whole story.

Thirdly, listening to the **context**, to identify assumptions you might be making about what is being said and to ask relevant clarifying questions.

Fourthly, listening to the **unsaid.** What has the speaker omitted and why might this be important?

Finally, listening for the **meaning** is critical to deep listening. All of these aspects contribute to the meaning. Integrating the five levels helps us to understand. Being open to listen in this way requires a respect for the speaker and the humility to listen deeply.

Oscar, who is passionate about the power of listening, describes conflict, chaos and confusion as the costs of *not listening*. Social cooperation, on which all societies and organisations are built, require us to play a non-zero-sum game. A hawk will fight another hawk, but it is not threatened by a dove. The cooperative endeavour of your career requires both courage and respect.

REFERENCES

[33] Barczewski, S. *Titanic: A Night Remembered.* London: Hambledon Continuum, 2006.

[34] Langley Research Centre. "Engineer Who Opposed Challenger Launch Offers Personal Look at Tragedy", NASA, 5 October 2012. [Online]. Available: https://www.nasa.gov/centers/langley/news/researchernews/rn_Colloquium1012.html. [Accessed 1 April 2021].

[35] Aristotle. "Rhetoric", MIT, 350 BCE.

[36] Curry, O.S., Mullins, D.A., and Whitehouse, H. "Is It Good to Cooperate?", *Current Anthropology,* vol. 60, no. 1, Feb 2019.

[37] Groysberg, B. *Chasing Stars: The myth of talent and the portability of performance.* Princeton, New Jersey: Princeton University Press, 2010.

[38] Kram, K. *Mentoring at Work: Developmental Relationships in Organisational Life.* Glenview, Illinois: Scott Foresman, 1985.

[39] Trimboli, O. *Deep Listening: Impact beyond words.* Sydney: oscartrimboli.com, 2017.

CHAPTER 10

EMPATHY

EMPATHY

ANALYSE CONNECTIONS

In the 1990s Kevin Bacon showed us that human connections are not random. 'Six degrees of Kevin Bacon' became a popular game to find the connections between apparently random strangers. It seems we're all connected somehow. Even so, research reported by the Australian Broadcasting Corporation (ABC) shows that less than half of Australians actually know their neighbours by name. Physical proximity doesn't automatically create connection. Connection needs to be cultivated.[40]

Workplaces can suffer from the same invisible barriers, despite physical proximity. People pass in the hall every day, but never speak to each other. People sit only metres apart, but never have a conversation. People know each other by sight, but not by name.

During the global coronavirus pandemic, periods of lockdown brought local communities closer together. People looked out for their neighbours, to check if they were okay, and perhaps spoke with them for the first time. Some streets had 'driveway drinks', children made chalk drawings on the footpaths and others left teddy bears in the windows for kids to spot while out for their walks. In a time of crisis, people made an effort to create meaningful connections. It shouldn't take a crisis for us to put effort into nurturing connections.

To empower your career, you need to nurture your connections right from the beginning. This will create learning opportunities and the networks that you will need as you progress in your career. As a leader you need to be deliberate about creating opportunities for engagement, whether that's in person or online. To engage your team and to empower them to engage others, connections need to be cultivated, not left to random chance.

You can use your analytical skills, already developed through analysing evidence and risks, to analyse connections. You can take a methodical approach to prioritising which connections to cultivate and plan deliberate action to establish and nurture connections, just as you do with any other planning process.

How are you cultivating connection?

BEING IGNORED IS WORSE THAN BEING REJECTED

In some ways, the rise of remote work has been a boon for engagement. It has meant that conversations must be scheduled and therefore may become more regular, rather than random. You may be able to see everyone on the screen at once, but it's harder to have a chat off to the side. It's not the same as the spontaneous interactions that can take place when we meet and mingle face to face.

As video meetings have boomed, most of us have spent quite a bit of time on them. I'm sure, like me, you've had the experience of talking away about something only to discover that you're still on mute. You've tried to convey your message, but nobody heard you. Unfortunately, this also can happen with in-person conversations. It's easy to feel ignored and that despite your best efforts, you're not getting traction with the people you're trying to engage. It's like talking on mute.

In many ways being ignored feels worse than being rejected. If people are willing to hear you out, consider your idea and give productive feedback, then you have the opportunity to tweak your ideas and bring them back for a second consideration. This is a lot more positive than if they're not even willing to listen at all. We all like the chance to be unmuted from time to time.

The etiquette of video calls is that you can unmute yourself while you speak, but when you're finished, you need to mute yourself again and listen to the next speaker. The same applies to real life interactions. If you find that you're being ignored, the first step is to stop and listen. Talking on mute is a waste of everyone's time, but muting ourselves to listen first, before we take our turn to speak, makes it more likely that our message will be heard.

Likewise, to nurture connections, we have to ensure we don't ignore others. If you understand how it feels to be ignored, you can put yourself in another person's shoes and realise that they might want to be included in the conversation. If you're developing a proposal or introducing a new idea, people who haven't been consulted may reject the proposal outright, regardless of its technical merits, just because they're disgruntled by being left out of the conversation.

Asset management touches every part of the organisation and involves both internal and external stakeholders. Therefore, it can be easy to leave someone out if we don't carefully think through who we need to engage. When I work with companies on developing their stakeholder engagement strategies, I ask two key questions.

The first is:

Who are your stakeholders?

So that you don't leave anyone out, you need to step carefully through all the touchpoints of your work and who it might impact. Consider who you may have overlooked. Rather than naming generic groups of stakeholders, such as 'suppliers' or 'regulators', it's useful to identify specific individuals and to write down their names.

Instead of just 'HR' or 'Legal', name the person you need to engage with in this area. Once you have a specific person in mind, it's much easier to put yourself in their shoes and take the time to understand their perspective. For example, how do they prefer to engage and what are their other priorities? As human beings we relate well to other human beings but less so to inanimate labels.

Once you've identified your important stakeholders, the second question to ask is:

What do they value?

The question is not, 'What do they value about you (or your proposal)?' The question is, 'What do they value?' Your area of interest may not even be on their radar, but knowing what's important to them will help you to establish and nurture your relationship with that person. It's also valuable to ask yourself, 'What do they need from me?' and 'How can I help them?'

LEAD WITH WARMTH, FOLLOW WITH COMPETENCE

In 2012, I had the great privilege to participate in an Executive Education program at Harvard Business School, where the inspirational Amy Cuddy was one of our professors.

Amy asked us an important question: 'Would you rather be liked, or be respected?'

A lot of professional people will say that they'd rather be respected. We are wary of appearing incompetent and eager to prove our worth. Among the 60 people in the room that day, 'I'd rather be respected' was the unanimous response. Amy's message to us was that if people don't like you first, they won't care what you have to say. You'll have no opportunity to earn their respect. You'll be ignored. One of the most important lessons I learned at Harvard was to lead with warmth, then follow with competence.

It's easy to spend a lot of time getting your facts right in order to prove a point. Of course, we don't want to get our facts wrong and having technically valid answers is important, but people connect first as human beings. It's your human qualities that are essential for building trust and nurturing connections.

Only once that trust is established, through a warm connection, will people be interested in what you have to say. You'll then have an opportunity to earn their respect through the quality of your work. As you journey through your career, it's the warmth of your connections, not the validity of your equations, that will give you the most long-term influence.

How are you leading with warmth?

Conversation is action

Talk may be cheap, but it's also enormously valuable.

Conversation is often underrated and can even be seen as 'a waste of time' that prevents us from 'taking action'. We've all heard exasperated people saying that we need to 'stop talking and get on with it.' However, the very human art of conversation is an essential part of leading with warmth.

When I was at Harvard Business School, I enjoyed a number of sessions led by Professor Boris Groysberg. In their book *Talk, Inc*, he and co-author Michael Sind share their research on organisational conversations. From their interviews with more than one hundred organisations, they describe conversations as the fuel that 'keeps the engine of value creation firing'.[41]

This research shows that far from being a waste of time, conversation increases trust, improves motivation and enhances employee commitment. The outcome is higher, rather than lower, operational productivity.

During the pandemic we had a need to keep physical distance, which reduced opportunities for the spontaneous conversations that usually arise in the workplace. These conversations are still essential, and the benefits can still be realised even if we can't meet face to face. However, it requires people to be motivated to take the time to engage.

Rather than being a barrier to action, conversation *is* action. It's important that we make a deliberate effort to decrease our metaphorical distance and engage in conversation. As leaders, we need to provide opportunities for our people to talk with us, and to talk with each other.

Who are you conversing with today?

Email is not engagement

It can be very tempting to default to email as our main means of communication, especially if we are working from home. It gives us time to think through what we'll say and edit where necessary. Email is useful where documents need to be exchanged and edits need to be made, but to pretend that email is engagement is like pretending that plastic fruit is edible. It may look good, but it won't do the job.

I remember a conversation with a client who had been struggling to implement an updated policy. They were frustrated that there had been no action or response, despite it having been almost two years since the change. When I asked what they had done to communicate these changes or engage people in taking action, it transpired that an email—singular—had been sent two years previously. Having had no response, nothing further had happened.

Many busy managers and executives have hundreds, if not thousands, of emails in their inbox at any one time. Simply sending an email and hoping someone will take action is rarely effective. Engagement needs to be synchronous, rather than asynchronous. There must be live dialogue, not just disconnected messages going back and forth. Engagement also needs to be rich, combining multiple channels that acknowledge the different ways the people prefer to communicate. Using a single channel for a single message is unlikely to inspire people to action.

Whether it's by video or in person, eyeballing each other is an important part of generating warm connections. Talking over the phone is also more valuable than sending a written document alone. One of the reasons that podcasts and audio books are so popular is that the warmth of a human voice creates greater connection than words alone.

Value is created through connection, not in isolation

James Gleick in his book *The Information* talks about the introduction of the electric telegraph. Gleick says that in 1852, the 'idea of connecting Europe with America, by lines extending directly across the Atlantic, is utterly impracticable and absurd'. The impossible was accomplished by 1858.[42]

Information that just two years earlier had taken days to arrive at its destination could now be there—anywhere—in seconds. This was not a doubling or tripling of transmission speed; it was a leap of many orders of magnitude.

Using this new technology, Queen Victoria exchanged pleasantries with USA President Buchanan. The *New York Times* announced, 'a result so practical, yet so inconceivable'.[42] The social consequences could not have been predicted, but some were observed and appreciated almost immediately. Fire brigades and police stations linked their communications. Proud shopkeepers advertised their ability to take telegraph orders. It was like the bursting of a dam whose presence has not even been known.

A telephone is useless if you don't know anyone else who has one. Who would you call? Sometimes we feel like we have to have all the answers—but we don't learn anything by talking to ourselves. It's only by looking outside our own environment that we can identify opportunities. We create real value when we make connections.

Collaboration requires a safe space

It's not enough to make connections, we need to make the most of them. Collaboration is critical to actively engaging and creating value through the connections we make. It's no use connecting the call if we don't have a conversation.

I worked with a company that was going through a re-structure and had a major building project underway to create a purpose-built workspace for their newly created team. This included a fancy new open plan office which was supposed to 'enhance collaboration'. By bringing everybody together into a single space, rather than the separate offices they currently had, it was hoped that there'd be more open communication between work groups and that this would support collaboration and innovation.

While there was some attempt at consultation on the design of the new space, the people who would go into the new office were spread across multiple floors of more than one building. The consultation process involved posting printed copies of plans on a wall in the corridor of one of these buildings, but not in the other buildings used by the company. It meant that for people in the other buildings to have an input into the consultation, they would have to leave their own building and go to another building where they may not normally have any reason to go.

Unsurprisingly, the teams in the other buildings felt ignored. They didn't feel that they had really been consulted or given a realistic opportunity for input. This barrier to the consultation process stifled collaboration. When the company moved to the new office, they no longer had physical walls between them, but the cultural barriers between teams still existed. These barriers had in fact been reinforced by the way the change was managed. It was amazing to see that those people who didn't speak to each other before the move, still didn't speak to each other afterward. There was no conscious action to create collaboration beyond the construction of the physical space. The physical walls had been replaced by 'invisible' walls, like a mime walking their hands up an imagined pane of glass.

Changing the physical environment can be beneficial, but we want to create value, not just artifacts. Collaboration requires a safe space, not just an open space. Unless people feel comfortable engaging with one another, the benefits won't be realised. For collaboration to be purposeful it requires a conscious decision and deliberate effort to bring people together who might normally just pass in the hall.

What are you doing to create a safe space for collaboration?

Collaboration requires structure

My Mum is a Girl Guide leader, and she taught me from a young age how to lay a fire that could be lit using no more than two matches, and which would definitely burn all night. On a trip we took together to Switzerland, we stayed at a Girl Guides Chalet where some Boy Scouts were visiting for a traditional campfire. The scouts had tried unsuccessfully to get the fire started. So, naturally we stepped in.

Instead of a haphazard pile of wood, we built a council fire, which is structured as a square-based pyramid, with alternate layers of sticks in each direction. Once the fire was lit it continued to burn through the layers, leaving wonderful coals for our marshmallows later in the evening.

Like a good fire, collaboration needs structure if the ideas are to burn beyond a spark. Valuable ideas aren't created in a vacuum, rather they emerge from within a cultural context and have their foundation in existing knowledge. Beyond the serendipity of random interactions, a structured collaborative process can help to build on these foundations, rather than discard them. As well as requiring a safe space, collaboration needs to be structured to make the most of collective learning, both past and present.

The aspects of structure that you can build into collaborative opportunities include the purpose, objectives, timing, venue, participants and agenda. Setting a structure doesn't mean limiting ideas: it means giving them fuel for their fire.

Effective collaboration is seamless

Most percussion drums are made with plies of wood that are inserted into a mould and joined together with glue. This creates layers in the drum shell, warping of the wood, and seams of weakness in the drum's integrity, which reduce its sound quality.

The best drums are made from a single piece of wood. This allows the drum to have a relaxed vertical grain, with no warping, no glue and no layers. These drums have a lower fundamental pitch, a cleaner tone and greater projection. A whole set of drums can be made from concentric circles of wood from the same log. This is rare, but highly sought after by drummers.

Like a quality drum shell, quality collaboration is seamless. Instead of layers of glue, there is no visible join. You need to reduce the barriers to collaboration—not just physical barriers, but also those cultural barriers that make a person feel unwelcome or unwilling to share their ideas. You can reduce these barriers by creating teams which have their own common purpose, regardless of where the people who are collaborating have come from. When collaborating across internal teams or across companies, create a fresh identity for the collaboration to give the team unity and a seamless approach. Be aware of where the barriers, visible or invisible, may arise.

How can you make your collaboration seamless?

Stakeholder engagement is never 'done'

We know that asset management touches the whole organisation, but it is also an embedded business discipline, not a one-off project. Your asset management system is not something that you build, then walk away from.

Do you remember the last time you bought a car? Did it come with oil already in the engine? Did you think that you'd never have to worry about oil again, because that had been 'done'? Probably not! Engine lubrication is not a one-off activity. We know we need to top up the oil or the engine will seize up.

It's the same with stakeholder engagement. It's not a one-off activity. Yet, when I'm working with asset management teams, I often hear them say that they've 'done' stakeholder engagement. There's a sense that it was something they had to tick off and they don't need to do it again. It's talked about in the past tense.

Like oil in your car, stakeholder engagement has to be ever present, or the good work you've already done will seize up. The value you've promised won't be delivered if all the parts don't move smoothly together.

Engagement needs to start right at the beginning of your asset management journey. Once you've begun, it's not enough to tick a box and say it's done.

Stakeholder engagement is never 'done'.

What are you doing each day to engage your stakeholders?

How do you keep the connections warm and positive?

Like your other Leadership Assets, empathy needs to be nurtured and practised over time so that it comes naturally. Developing habits around how you engage with people in your workplace and more broadly, helps you to build this capability. Making the effort to get to know people and nurture warm connections will empower your career for years to come.

REFERENCES

[40] Hartley, A. "Coronavirus sparks first real conversations with neighbours after years of living next door", *ABC News,* no. 02 April 2020.

[41] Groysberg, B. and Slind, M. *Talk, Inc.* Boston: Harvard Business School Publishing, 2012.

[42] Gleick, J. *The Information.* London: Harper Collins, 2011.

CHAPTER 11

INTEGRITY

INTEGRITY

CREATE MEANING

In geometry, two shapes are congruent if they have the same shape and size, or if the shape and size of one is the mirror image of the other. The shapes can be rotated or flipped to match, but if re-sizing is required, they're not congruent.

Recently, we had a family sewing bee. My daughter was inspired to make a new dress and we had bought a pattern and some lovely fabric. We spent a day with Nana, my sister and a bunch of cousins and it was lots of fun. To cut the required pieces of fabric to make the dress, we first had to fold the fabric in half. Placing the pattern on the fabric and cutting when folded produces two congruent pieces. They're not identical, but they fit together, creating the right and left side of the garment. If you cut the pieces separately, you can end up with a mismatch, where the pattern in the fabric doesn't line up, or there is a gap, which means the clothing won't fit.

Just like the pieces of fabric in a garment, our statements and our actions need to be congruent. Doing what we say we will do is the definition of integrity. Whenever we try to act in conflict with our stated beliefs, we suffer what Aristotle spoke of as cognitive dissonance. To us, it's uncomfortable, like ill-fitting clothing. To others, it's hypocrisy—the patterns don't line up.

We might think that the way to resolve this discomfort would be to change our actions to fit our beliefs. However, landmark research by

Festinger and Carlsmith in 1959, which has been verified by many subsequent studies, showed that the opposite is often true.[43] Such is the drive to resolve the dissonance we feel that we will change our beliefs to justify actions we've already taken. This may make us feel more comfortable in our clothing, but the patterns still don't match.

Integrity is a concept that asset managers are familiar with when it comes to assets. Structural integrity, mechanical integrity, systems integrity are all things that we deal with on a day-to-day basis.

How do we extend this concept to demonstrate human integrity?

MAKING MEANING IS WHAT MAKES US HUMAN

As the pandemic played havoc with sporting schedules and events around the world were cancelled, we were fortunate in Australia that some sporting activities could go ahead, under restricted and modified conditions. One such sport was the Australian Football League (AFL) which is a popular football variation unique to Australia with a rich and storied history. Part of that history is the AFL's Victorian origins and that regardless of where the teams may come from, the grand final is always played on the hallowed turf of the Melbourne Cricket Ground (MCG), deemed to be the spiritual home of the AFL.

Due to the impact of COVID and restrictions in force in Melbourne, much of the AFL season was played interstate, with players and officials isolated into bubbles. As the grand final time grew closer, it became apparent that holding it at the MCG wasn't going to be an option. The grand final was instead played—between two

Victorian teams—at the Brisbane Cricket Ground in Queensland, affectionately known as the 'Gabba'.

The logistics of such an event are immense, but as part of the preparations, a square of grass from the MCG was rolled up, put onto a refrigerated truck and transported about 1800 km to Brisbane. This turf was transplanted into the ground at the Gabba in time for the grand final. The effort and expense of this gesture had no practical role: it was purely symbolic. It was a gesture laden with meaning that recognises our human yearning for connection to people and to place. The gesture drew criticism from some, saying that it was a waste of money in difficult times and these funds could have been better spent elsewhere, such as in supporting grassroots sport.

There are arguments on both sides, highlighting that it's the meaning we draw from an action, rather than the action itself, that is often most significant. Meaning is created in the context of our connection with other human beings. Like an electrical circuit, energy only flows when the connection is complete. It's important that the meaning we create reflects integrity, a oneness with those we seek to connect.

A strategy should not be an unsolvable mystery

Alignment is one of the fundamentals of asset management. Part of what it requires is that there's alignment between the asset management activities of a company and its overall strategic objectives. However, alignment is not a one-way street. Developing a viable corporate strategy requires that an understanding of the organisation be part of the context in which that strategy is developed.

Outsold only by the Bible, Agatha Christie's crime novels have sold over two billion copies. For fiction written in English, only Shakespeare comes close in total sales, but he had a four-hundred-year head start. In more than eighty novels, Agatha Christie held readers in suspense as they tried to use their 'little grey cells' to deduce the villain in a series of nasty murders. Over the years, many theories have emerged that seek to explain the secret to Christie's success.

The 2005 documentary, *The Agatha Christie Code*,[44] told how text analysis was used to try to explain some of the mysteries of Christie's famed stories. Cognitive science recognises that the conscious human mind can only respond to a limited number of inputs at one time. Princeton University psychologist Professor George Miller in a 1956 paper claimed that this number was seven, plus or minus two. In theory it means that no one can hold more than nine ideas simultaneously in their conscious mind.[45] In *The Agatha Christie Code*, the theory proposed was that Agatha Christie always had at least ten threads to her stories.[44] This meant that it was impossible for the reader to keep track of them all—a clever way to maintain the mystery and suspense.

Whether Agatha Christie consciously wrote in this way, we will probably never know. However, it's an important reminder of the need to be aware of the limitations of the conscious mind when designing your business strategy. More recent neuroscience suggests that Miller was optimistic and that the limit to processing capacity is more likely three to five items.[45]

Having a 55-point plan for growth might be fantastic, but nobody can remember all the points. To be effective, strategy needs to be internalised.

Recently, I worked with a client to narrow their focus areas down to six. In fact, the second three are a mirror of the first three, so there are really only three to remember. Everybody in the company can internalise these three things and everyone can apply them to their daily work. In practice, this means you should limit your areas of focus to no more than five. In asset management we need to translate the corporate strategy into actionable plans that make sense to people and can be readily followed. There's really no future for a strategy that can't be comprehended by the conscious mind.

The strategy you internalise is the only strategy you have

I once attended a concert of fantastic contemporary music for choir and two pianos. There is nothing quite like watching a live concert pianist at work. For two pianists to play simultaneously and keep the harmony and rhythm in sync is very challenging, but amazing to watch when it's done well.

What you notice about professional musicians is that they play the music from memory. Performing great music is about more than just playing the notes. Not only have they memorised the score, but they've internalised the music, its nuances and its meaning, so that they can tell the composer's story with passion and energy.

When we see people perform in the business world, there's often a disconnect between what the composer has written in the score and what the player performs on the stage. We feel the dissonance and we know it lacks integrity. Strategies and plans may be written down, but not internalised. Systems and processes may be cumbersome, overly complex and unwieldy to implement. Musicians can memorise music because music has patterns and harmonies that make sense. Music is not a random collection of disjointed notes.

Likewise, in asset management your strategies and plans need to make sense. They need to be in harmony with your vision and values and clear enough for everyone to internalise. A random hotchpotch of systems and processes that don't work together or don't work towards the overall vision will never help the business progress and will inevitably be abandoned while people revert to playing the tunes they know.

If you want your organisation to perform at its best, you need to design your systems the way a composer writes music, with an overall vision for the story to be told, with patterns and themes that fit that vision and with harmonies that make sense. The notes aren't separate to the music—they are integral to it. This is what alignment and integrity are all about.

I often hear people refer to 'the strategy piece' as something they are doing, working on or waiting for. Strategy, however, is not 'a piece': it is the integrated essence of the whole. Just as you can't have half a raw egg, you can't have a 'piece' of strategy. Be wary if you're asked to work on a piece without understanding the whole or the overall picture. It's essential for everyone, from the board room to the workshop floor, to have a common view of how their actions contribute to the desired outcomes. While delegation is essential to ensuring tasks are completed, delegation in itself does not ensure integration.

Delegation is not integration

The 'Oarsome Foursome' were an Australian Olympic and World Champion rowing team, competing most famously as a coxless four. Through the 1990s and into the early 2000s they were an unbeatable team and hugely popular in Australia.

One of the essentials of a winning rowing team is that they all row together, in the same direction, at the same time. They don't 'divvy it up'. Imagine if the coach decided to delegate: OK Nick, you go forwards; Mike, you go backwards; Sam, you go left; James, you go right. Instead of winning the race, they'd just go around and around in circles.

Delegation is not integration. When tasks are divided up between managers who aren't working together, they're no longer whole-of-organisation objectives. This approach can perpetuate silos and be a barrier to true integration.

When we talk about alignment as an asset management fundamental, or in any management context, it's not just about a vertical alignment between organisational objectives and functional plans. It's also about horizontal alignment—across teams, across functions and across stakeholder groups.

How do you create opportunities for transdisciplinary collaboration?

How do you ensure that you have integration, not just delegation?

How do you ensure that you're all rowing together?

LEADERSHIP INTEGRITY

In an address at the National War College on December 19, 1952, United States President Harry Truman said, "You know, it's easy for the Monday morning quarterback to say what the coach should have done after the game is over. But when the decision is up before you - and on my desk I have a motto which says 'the buck stops here' - the decision has to be made."[47]

You can't blame the people below you

Leadership and culture are determinants of value. It's critical for leaders to take responsibility for value creation and to 'set the tone from the top'. A board, like the President, has nobody else to pass the buck to. Leadership overarches all of the roles of the board and is one of the fundamentals of asset management, as defined in the ISO 55001 international standards for asset management.

The aim of asset management is to create value for stakeholders through the organisation's assets. While technical systems and processes may be in place, without effective leadership, value creation will be limited. Stakeholder expectations will drive many aspects of asset management decision making. Working with and through the CEO, the board has a crucial leadership role in engaging with relevant internal and external stakeholders, setting expectations, and monitoring and reviewing performance.

Important questions for the board to ask about its leadership role in asset management:

- Does our workplace culture support effective asset management practices?
- Is there good communication between the relevant areas of the business?
- Is each person clear on the nature of their role and responsibilities?
- Do we have the appropriate people employed in critical roles?

- How do we engage with stakeholders to ensure timely consultation on relevant asset management issues?

Boards make collective decisions. It's different to executive decision making. This is an important nuance to understand if you're in a board role, or if you're presenting a proposal to the board. From this perspective, it means that you have more than one person to convince.

In my experience as a chairman, I've always aimed to work towards consensus in the decisions of the board. It's important to listen to the dissenting voice. It's important to have a robust discussion and to hear different points of view. If the board can't come to a consensus, based on the information provided in your proposal, they may ask you for further information. This could be to provide greater depth, or to add context and relevance. It means the process may take longer than you'd like, but the additional information will help the board come to a decision that best balances risk and opportunity.

The messenger is as important as the message

Diana, Princess of Wales, was renowned for her fashion choices. Top designers around the world clamoured to make dresses for her. These designers knew that their dress, worn by Diana, would achieve 'money can't buy' media coverage. They also knew that while Diana would look good in their design, more importantly, their design would look amazing on her.

A few years ago, I visited Kensington Palace, which was once Diana's home, to view an exhibition of her dresses. While these haute couture gowns are works of art in their own right, the dress hanging on a mannequin was unremarkable when compared with the photo of Diana wearing the same dress.

Although the dress is a three-dimensional, tangible object, the flat two-dimensional photo conveys more life and energy than the dress itself. It's intangible and yet so valuable. These dresses now fetch astronomical prices at charity auctions, not because of who designed them, but because of who wore them.

Great care and attention went into the outfits worn by Diana. Jasper Conran, who designed numerous pieces for Diana's working wardrobe, recalls that whenever the Princess tried anything on, she would always ask 'What message am I giving out in this?'[47]

When you're trying to convey a message, it's not enough to have a beautifully conceived technical concept and robust data to back it up. Sometimes we spend so long getting the design 'right' that we forget about who's wearing it.

For your message to shine, it needs more than a material structure. It needs *you*, to give it energy and bring it to life. Your personal integrity is essential to this. How are you perceived by those to whom you're delivering your message? Are you seen as a trusted advisor? Are you seen to be engaged in the strategic dialogue, or are you focused on the technical details?

How does your message look on you?

PEOPLE ARE NOT ASSETS

A common catchcry of many organisations, and their leaders, is that 'people are our greatest assets'. I cringe every time I hear this. As leaders it is not acceptable to treat our people like machines, or mere economic artefacts. There's a value exchange between a person and their employer, whereby that person contributes their skill and effort to the aims of the enterprise and is rewarded with remuneration and other benefits. At no time does the organisation own that person. People are not commodities to be exploited. Instead, they are human beings with real feelings and emotions, real lives and real futures.

Of course, we need to value our people, but putting them on the balance sheet alongside buildings and equipment, as some would advocate, isn't the way to do that. Defining a person's worth by their monetary 'value' does both the person and their organisation a gross disservice.

It's essential that we, as leaders in asset management, don't fall into the trap of dropping people into our asset management system as if they were just another piece of kit. The technical approach and the business perspective are necessary, but not sufficient. Machines are expendable, but people are not. Human integrity defines our leadership. Having the humility to understand the priorities of others, the empathy to connect on a human level, and a focus on creating real meaning for our people and our communities are essential qualities of any leader.

Leadership isn't for everyone. If you choose to pursue a leadership journey, your human qualities will be the most critical to determining if the journey is a fulfilling and rewarding one and that you'll be a leader worth following.

REFERENCES

[43] Cooper, J. and Karlsmith, K.M. "Cognitive Dissonance", in International Encyclopedia of the Social and Behavioural Sciences, Amsterdam, Elselvier, 2001.

[44] The Agatha Christie Code. [Film]. Screened on ABC Television, 2006.

[45] Miller, G. "The magical number seven, plus or minus two: Some limits on our capacity for processing information", Psychological Review, vol. 63, pp. 81-97, 1956.

[46] Parker, G. "Acta is a four letter word", Acta Psychiatrica Scandinavica, 17 August 2012.

[47] Truman, H.S., President. Address at the National War College. [Sound Recording]. U.S. Army Signal Corps, 1952.

[48] Wilkes, D. "Princess Diana's scarlet Jasper Conran suit that was bought at auction for GBP50,000 goes on public display for the first time to showcase her unique style of 'tradition with a twist'", Daily Mail, 1 February 2020.

CASE STUDIES

CASE STUDIES

As asset management matures as a recognised professional discipline, those working in asset management will seek clarity on available career paths and guidance on the development needed to pursue these potential pathways. A formal qualification may be the entry point into the profession, but this will be augmented throughout a person's career with further industry-specific formal training, on-the-job learning, and formal or informal mentoring.

This chapter presents a series of case studies based on interviews I undertook with asset management professionals at different stages of their careers. It was a qualitative approach using semi-structured, one-on-one interviews with leaders and emerging leaders at various organisational levels. Those interviewed shared experiences from their career journey and reflected on how different learning opportunities had impacted their career choices, their leadership development, and ultimately their progression in their asset management careers.

These case studies show that rather than a single, defined, or linear pathway, a core set of capabilities are associated with career progression in asset management. These include technical capabilities, business capabilities and interpersonal capabilities. They illustrate how these capabilities can be nurtured throughout the stages of a career in asset management through a combination of formal and informal professional development.

While foundational qualifications focus largely on development of technical and, to some extent, business knowledge and skills, managerial capabilities can be developed through on-the-job learning and postgraduate or industry-based training. While some communication skills can be taught in a structured learning context, capabilities needed for effective leadership may best be cultivated through strong formal or informal mentoring relationships.

At all times, but especially in a time of economic restraint, it's important that individuals and organisations invest their time and their resources in development activities that create value both for the individuals themselves and for the organisations they work with.

The case studies offer insights into potential career pathways for leaders in asset management, and highlight the capabilities required to pursue these pathways. These insights are valuable to leaders and potential leaders at all stages—those who seek to progress their asset management careers, those who lead organisations, and those who develop the leaders of the future.

OBJECTIVE

I aimed to explore the diversity of career paths in asset management, through a series of case studies within a single company.

I sought to map the career development pathways of a group of established and emerging leaders within that company, and to determine what they perceived to be the relative importance for their career journey of three development methods: formal training, on-the-job learning, and mentoring. I wanted to find out, from the personal stories of individuals, how these different development approaches had shaped their pathways.

I explored these development approaches within the context of three core capability areas seen to be essential for successful engineering leaders: technical capabilities, business/management capabilities, and communication capabilities. I chose these capability areas based on industry frameworks and the company's internal leadership development framework.

Names have been changed for anonymity.

METHODS

Organisation Background

The company is a service provider in the mining industry. The business area from which the case studies are drawn is responsible for asset management, with the primary assets being heavy mining equipment and fixed processing plants. The asset management group is involved in every stage of the asset management life cycle, from equipment selection and acquisition through its operational life to its ultimate disposal.

Case Study Approach

A qualitative approach was taken using semi-structured, one-on-one interviews with five individuals within the company. I chose these methods in order to observe real and complex situations, in the settings in which they occur. Each person was at a different stage of their leadership journey and at different levels of formal authority within the organisation.

Using the semi-structured format, I set a number of questions for the interviews, while others arose during the interview itself. The interview structure centred around the main themes of:

- Leadership capabilities: technical, business, communication
- Leadership development approaches: formal training, on-the-job learning, mentoring
- Leadership pathways: past development opportunities and future aspirations
- Leadership examples: role models and mentors both within engineering and more broadly.

Each interview lasted about one hour and was recorded on a digital voice recorder and transcribed using a professional transcription service. I also took hand-written notes during the interview.

Responses to set questions were categorised and transcript anecdotes were used to develop a narrative case for each participant.

I mapped the leadership development pathways of the three senior participants using a standard organisational chart of the company under study, but representative of other companies the participant may have worked with.

CASE STUDY 1: ROBIN – EXECUTIVE MANAGER

Formal Training and Experience

Robin is currently the Executive Manager, Plant. He has been with the company for four-and-a-half years and during that time has held a number of positions within this business area. Robin's initial qualifications were as a process instrument mechanic, and he spent 21 years with an oil and gas company. He held various positions in other organisations before joining this company. Apart from his apprenticeship, Robin completed seven years of formal post-trade training up to certificate level and various industry-based management and leadership training programs. To complement his management experience, Robin also completed an MBA.

The masters was invaluable….from a confidence perspective….and it gave me some frames and models to use and also validated the gut feel.

Leadership Pathway

Robin can trace his leadership pathway back to his days as an apprentice, although at that time his ambitions were modest.

I started off as an apprentice and my goal in being an apprentice was to become a tradesman. My goal in life being a tradesman was to become a supervisor.

After a supervisor, I actually didn't have any real progressive aspirations, I didn't have many good role models.

Robin's idea of leadership and his potential pathways changed when, as a supervisor, he worked with the person he describes as *still the most inspirational leader that I have worked for.* At this point

Robin was offered a promotion that set him on a path away from a focus on the technical aspects of his trade and into people management. As a shop steward involved with the enterprise bargaining process, he recognised that he had an interest in working with people.

It became more apparent to me because other people recognised it.

Robin identified that his people skills became more important than his technical skills in terms of the respect he commands as a leader.

Well, my technical skills are now obsolete. [My current role] it's not a technical role, but....I could do any one of ten people roles in the organisation.

Robin identified a number of people who stood out as having been role models for him in his life.

As an apprentice, one of the tradesmen said, 'Come with me son and I'll teach you a trade'. *[He] trusted me and taught me how to be a tradesman, rather than just showing me. There's a subtlety in that.*

Later, a supervisor Robin worked with identified that his moods could sometimes affect his work.

He talked to me about being mindful of my moods and what causes it, and that, in those days, was unheard of.

There was another tradesman who influenced Robin because of his technical brilliance.

No matter what I do to this day, I look and think, what would [he] be doing?

Another manager set a bad example for Robin and taught him what to avoid as a manager.

[He] taught me all about being the absolute control freak and what not to be in a manager. Every time I think I'm being a bad manager I score myself against [him].

Views on Leadership

For Robin the key characteristics that make a good leader are:

Vision; the innate ability to paint a picture in a story.

Don't compromise your value.

[Leaders need to give people] room to be themselves and to grow. A good leader should be able to adapt...to their situation.

Robin estimated that on balance 20% of his professional development has come from formal training, while 80% would have been on-the-job.

Coaching and mentoring have been a huge part of my learning.

Stories were an important part of this—an important mentor used stories as a teaching tool.

It's easier to use stories from the past that people have lived through. Taking people on a journey and building a team is what I've been doing. I actually draw back on my library of stories, adapt them for the audience I'm with, or manipulate them, and then tell the story.

Overall, Robin's view of leadership is centred on the idea of being a coach or mentor.

My view of leadership is very much about how you enable people to reach their potential.

CASE STUDY 2: BARRY – PLANT MANAGER

Formal Training and Experience

Barry is the Plant Manager for the Queensland region. He started his career as an apprentice mechanical fitter and has been with the company for 30 years, beginning as a fitter in the workshops.

I was the only fitter there in my fourth year. I'm a bit self-taught. [At that time] there was no such thing as a mechanical fitter where I was. So, I got my certificate as a fitter and turner.

Barry's career has included a wide range of infrastructure and mining projects. He says that beyond his apprenticeship, he's had very little other formal training.

They didn't have that sort of training in the early days, and when they did come on...they felt that I already had enough experience.

I'm very committed to the training process. Nowadays when graduates come on, they don't get the exposure to the field and plant because [on the project] they're always too busy to show them what to do.

Leadership Pathway

When Barry talks about his leadership pathway, he acknowledges it has been a learning journey.

I was very outspoken and have been told that I didn't always get certain jobs because I made too much noise. But I always believe in being yourself, and being honest, and being committed. That's how I got where I did.

From Barry's point of view, technical competence is important to building respect as a leader.

With all my life experience, you've got machines going wrong....and things and I just rattled off from memory, 'Well, that happened at such and such a job'.

Barry felt that his first-hand experience meant he was taken more seriously.

However, he also recognised that technical skills are necessary but not sufficient to be respected as a leader. Recounting an experience early in his career Barry says, *I spat the dummy here one day and screamed and yelled and carried on. I used to yell, scream, put people down. I learnt [that behaviour] very early, when I was in the position of being a leading hand. It took me to my mid-40s to realise that it does matter [how you treat people].*

In my current role, Robin has taught me a lot on how to deal with people in situations. [He's a] very good people manager. I admire him for that.

Views on Leadership

In Barry's opinion, relationships are really the key to leadership. After thirty years in the one company, he values the relationships that have been developed over that time. He feels that people who move from company to company don't necessarily develop the same type of deep relationships, both within the company and with suppliers. Barry believes that involving people is the key to good leadership.

I think that's the whole key, to work with the workers.

You've just got to befriend them—you don't have to be mates, pals—but you've got to interact.

Another relationship that Barry mentioned as being important was the relationship between asset management and operations. One operations manager Barry worked with took the time to *understand the plant side of things and he taught me about the earthworks side of things and how you should know each other's jobs.* Barry felt that this understanding strengthened the relationships and helped things run more smoothly.

Barry also saw setting a good example as an important leadership characteristic, especially in terms of safety and meeting required standards and regulations.

The rules and regulations are there, they've set the standard, stick by it. If you break the rules with one, well you've lost it [respect].

Barry sees that an important part of his leadership role is to pass his experience on to younger colleagues.

One thing that I try to do with....mentoring the apprentices....the hardest part I find is trying to pass that experience on to them, so that they don't have to learn a lot by their mistakes. I fell over a lot, if you know what I mean.

CASE STUDY 3: JIM – CIVIL ENGINEER

Formal Training and Experience

Jim is a civil engineer with over 30 years' experience in the industry. He has had two stints with this company, totalling almost 20 years. He began his career with a firm of consulting engineers where he was involved with a lot of survey work.

Jobs were pretty hard to find and work was very thin on the ground and I used the 'old boys' network'. Dad knew a bloke who was a partner in the consulting firm and so I ended up with a job in there.

Jim has held a range of roles across Australia and New Zealand in both mining and construction, including a period as project manager on a mining project. He is now the Technical Services Manager for the plant function within the mining business of the study company.

Leadership Pathway

About two years after graduating, Jim was seconded to a contracting company and really enjoyed it.

By that stage the job market had picked up…and I picked up a job with a construction contractor doing road building. I was the first engineer they'd ever hired, which was amazing, but it was all family. All the branches were managed by family members, and they'd all grown up from the bottom and learned it from the bottom end. So [the boss] had a philosophy that we'll train you the same way that I've trained everyone else. So, I got put into the business for six months and I spent six months in the asphalt plant, six months with the paving crews [and so on].

Jim felt that this practical experience was invaluable for his ability to deal with people.

It was just so much fun, and learning to work with people, normal crews. Working in that small business taught me so much about people, it was really something. Having worked driving machines, operating machines, shovelling and whatever, they don't see you as some shiny tail that has just come in.

Following his initial undergraduate studies, Jim returned to university twice more, firstly to study maths and then to start an MBA. In both cases Jim decided that his practical experience was more valuable than this formal training and didn't continue with the studies.

In terms of industry-based training, Jim has completed many of the required licences for different vehicles and equipment, as well as Workplace Health and Safety Officer training. He has now let that qualification lapse as moving from state to state made it too difficult to keep them up. He also believed that while an understanding of workplace health and safety is essential for a mine manager, there needs to be a separate person in that role, otherwise there is too much conflict.

In terms of mentors, Jim cites his father-in-law as an important influence.

I had absolutely no direction and I just started going out with my wife and her father took me aside and said, 'You seem to be a bright young lad. Where are you going?' He worked for the local Council and arranged for me to go and see the chief engineer and go and spend some time with the engineering and building and some of the transport sides, just to get exposed...that was fantastic.

Jim explained that at the consulting firm he first worked with, it was hard to 'click' with the other engineers because at that time everyone was still called 'Mr' instead of by their first names. Jim felt that there was a cultural divide. In a subsequent job a consulting engineer said, 'Call me Ken'.

Now, I still stay in touch with him and have all my life. He still works, he's 83 now, amazing guy. He's been an amazing mentor over the years. If ever I've had some challenging issues and I'm looking for guidance, I still go back to him.

Another important mentor for Jim was an electrician who was *ahead of his time in terms of his approach to safety. [At that time] we didn't have a single thing documented about what we did.*

Views on Leadership

You work for people, you don't work for the companies—good people are worth following. The fact that they're interested in you makes a heck of a difference. You can talk to them about anything at any time. They are consistent. They don't change their values—no matter what pressure they are under; those things will not change no matter what. That's really it.

The other thing [about people worth following] is that they would always welcome a different point of view. When I think back to these people, every single one of them you would feed off because you don't agree about everything all of the time. Having different views and approaches—then you get the best out of the situation. That would be consistent across all of the people I consider to be worthy of following or who mentored me.

Jim believes that the most important characteristic in a leader is the people every time. *You can get by with a technical understanding as opposed to a technical knowledge, but if you can't deal with people, or the people you're working for can't deal with their people, it's awkward.*

I remember a HR guy I worked with in Western Australia. [When we were working on a tender] this guy was putting together all of the plans around the HR and he would say to me, 'Nothing you are doing is going to shut this job down for a month' [but if something goes wrong with the HR].

CASE STUDY 4: LISA – GRADUATE ENGINEER

Lisa is a graduate in chemical engineering with a second degree in science. She also completed one year of her university studies in France, where there was a focus on nuclear energy, and the emphasis was highly technical. Lisa joined the company on graduation, but during her studies also completed vacation work at a number of other companies. As a high school student, she had experience working in retail.

Lisa has completed the first year of a two-year graduate program that involves rotations through various roles including periods in the head office, the regional office and on site.

Leadership Pathway

Lisa feels that in some ways she is a bit isolated, being a chemical engineer in a mechanical environment. She mentioned that Jim [Technical Services Manager, Case Study 3] has been good for that, because he's also not a mechanical engineer: *He always touches base, even when I'm on site.*

The main people Lisa has developed relationships with while on site have been operations-based leaders, such as project managers and mining engineers. She has maintained contact with these people through her different rotations whether on another site or back in the office, and they have been a good source of support.

When asked what her role was in the company, Lisa said that she didn't really know. *I'm learning from practice at this stage, dealing with operators who are not qualified but very experienced. This is a good learning experience, but I won't be willing to do site-based work forever. I'd like to go overseas, probably at a similar level at first, in a technical role, but then I will look to move away from the technical side to a more people-oriented role.*

Lisa didn't see further formal training as important to her future career development.

If I do further study, it will be for my own interest, because I enjoy it, rather than because it's essential to my progression.

As a woman, Lisa didn't feel that being female affected her day-to-day work; however, she felt that timeframes were important for her career pathway.

I want to have a family, so I need to get experience quickly and be at a reasonable level in order to take time out.

Views on Leadership

Among those leaders that Lisa has so far had the opportunity to work with, she feels that there are various characteristics that are important:

- They take in interest in you and what you are doing.
- They are inspiring and action oriented.
- They are happy to give responsibility.
- They see the big picture and make that picture clear to others.

In good leaders, listening is important. It leads to valuable decision making.

Undoubtedly people skills are the most important for leadership development, technical skills can be learned or asked and management skills will follow if the people skills are there.

I don't feel that there needs to be a formal situation for mentoring, but I need to know that people are there if I need them. You can learn a lot from the experience of others and experience is respected in this industry. You don't end up doing the job you studied for—you pick it up along the way.

CASE STUDY 5: TONY – APPRENTICE BOILERMAKER

Formal Training and Experience

Tony has just completed the first year of his boilermaker's apprenticeship. He is in his late twenties and was a chef for ten years before taking up this apprenticeship. When asked why he decided to become a boilermaker, Tony said, *I was sick of the hours being a chef, working weekends and nights—and then it was bad money and bad hours— I mean I may as well work bad hours and get paid for it. I think I like building stuff really, so I thought I'd enjoy it apart from anything else. I've never had any experience doing this at all so it's good but there's a lot of learning to be done.*

During the first year of his apprenticeship, apart from the three two-week blocks at college, Tony has completed a range of on-the-job training including a Forklift Ticket, Working at Heights, CPR, Fire Training and so on. *Anytime a new procedure comes through they usually grab eight or nine of us at a time and go through it, they're pretty thorough.*

Leadership Pathway

I suppose [here] everyone is a leader. Any of the tradesmen down there are pretty good. I suppose it's different with a mature age apprentice. I'm sure they would treat [people] the same regardless of age, but you know, they would feel more comfortable, [that you're not just] wasting your time, [or theirs]. I mean the boss here looks after us because he's a trainer but if they're walking past and you need to check something, any of them will come in and give you advice.

On a day-to-day basis Tony doesn't have much interaction with leaders outside his own workshop environment. However, earlier in the year he was involved in an incident investigation where he worked with Jim [Technical Services Manager, Case Study 3] and the Workshops Manager.

Tony has been happy with the training he's received here, especially with regards to safety. He feels that it's been very thorough. Tony said that the atmosphere is *easy going, but not lax. Everyone gets along well.*

When he's finished his apprenticeship, Tony would like a job as a boilermaker with the company. He doesn't feel that another company would look at him straight out of a trade. His view is that he will need about 10 years' experience with one company. At this stage he hasn't looked at career opportunities beyond the tradesman level.

His aim is to have a secure job so that he can buy a house and start a family. Those are his aims over the next ten years.

Views on Leadership

Tony believes that leaders need patience and understanding. In his previous role as a chef, he admired Gordon Ramsay for his dedication, focus and passion. *Leaders need to give guidance and that requires patience and perseverance. They need to know what they want.*

CONCLUSIONS

Every person interviewed in this study cited people skills as ultimately more important than technical skills for an effective leader. Even those in the early stages of their careers recognised that the technical skills gained through formal training, while important, were somewhat less important to their effectiveness in their current and potential future roles than their on-the-job experience. Technical skills would be developed through this experience but may be very different from the area of formal training undertaken. Ultimately, to move beyond a technical role and become a leader within their organisation or their profession, they needed to know how to deal with people, relate to people and manage people.

Leadership development begins at the undergraduate or apprentice level. There is an opportunity for those who develop and run formal training programs, in universities and other training organisations, to recognise the importance of communication and people skills to leadership development and to ensure that effective training in these skills is included in foundation courses. Leadership development should not be left to 'later in life'.

Both Robin and Barry, who are now in senior leadership roles, did not see the potential career path that was available to them when they were apprentices. The interview with Tony reveals that as an apprentice today, he also doesn't see the career path beyond his initial trade training. He hasn't been exposed to these opportunities or had interaction with the people who have pursued a leadership path from his current position. There is an opportunity for these senior leaders to share their leadership pathway stories with graduates and apprentices from an early stage, to help encourage and develop the leaders of the future.

Every person interviewed could name one or more mentors who had helped them develop their people skills, either through the direct intervention of the mentor or through active observation where the mentor set an example that they chose to follow. In some cases, mentor relationships were also important to the development of technical and business skills.

In these case studies, effective mentors were those who were able to identify the strengths and weaknesses of their protégé and communicate these to the person with courage, tact and insight. The mentor did not need to be in a formal position of authority over the protégé. Many of the mentor relationships described began early on and have spanned the person's whole career. There was some consistency between the generations with what were seen to be desirable characteristics in a leader. Jim said that taking an interest was important in those who mentored him, and he now uses those same skills as a mentor to others, including Lisa, who mentioned this as one of Jim's leadership strengths.

These case studies highlight the importance of establishing mentor relationships early in one's career. While these relationships may form spontaneously and be informal in nature, organisations can assist young people starting out in their careers by providing opportunities for mentor relationships to develop and by equipping their employees with the skills to identify their own strengths and weaknesses.

For experienced leaders or those new to leadership roles, organisations can ensure that they understand the importance of their role as a mentor, whether informally or formally. As a leader they set an example that others will follow, whether they are aware of it or not. Equipping emerging leaders with the skills to act as effective mentors and to identify mentoring opportunities will improve the development opportunities for less experienced employees and ensure that they have the capabilities to step up to leadership roles in the future.

QUESTIONS FOR LEADERS

- Does your company have a formal mentoring program?
- Are your leaders trained in coaching and mentoring skills?
- Do your current leaders actively identify emerging leaders and ensure that their potential is nurtured?
- Do your leaders share their own stories to enhance the development of future asset management leaders?

QUESTIONS FOR FUTURE LEADERS

- Have you considered your own pathway to leadership?
- What capabilities do you need to develop to follow your desired path?
- What approaches can you use to develop these capabilities?
- Do you have a formal or informal mentor?
- What types of mentors will be important to you in the future?
- How can you actively seek and develop these relationships?

NEXT STEPS

What's the next step for your career?

That depends on where you are now and what your ambitions are.

It's worthwhile doing a gap analysis on your own development to work out what the best next steps might be for you.

At the end of this section is a QR code which you can use to download a workbook to help you through this process.

FOR APPRENTICES

While your period as an 'apprentice' in asset management will focus on formal training, on-the-job learning is also really important. It's not too early to find a mentor. Identify the leaders that you look up to and seek them out. Ask your company if they provide a mentor as part of your development program.

Get involved in your professional body, attend their events and seminars, volunteer for a committee that takes your interest. Learn as much as you can and get to know people both inside and outside your company, to expand your professional networks.

Your formal training will focus mostly on technical skills, but now is the time to start developing those Biz Smarts and Street Smarts that you'll need for the future. Ask experienced people about their career journeys and learn from the challenges they've faced. People love to share 'war stories' and you can learn a lot from these.

FOR ADVISORS

By now you've got some experience under your belt and you're quite proficient in your technical skills. It's important at this stage to ensure you've got the Biz Smarts you'll need to operate at a leadership level. Once you are leading a team, or accountable for a budget, it's critical that you can connect your work and the work of your team to the company's overall strategic objectives. Make sure you understand these and that you can articulate the role you play.

This is a good time to consider whether there's any relevant postgraduate or industry-based training that will complement your technical skills.

Ensure you have a mentor who can help you navigate the next steps and also make sure that you are building networks beyond your current employer.

FOR ADVOCATES

By this stage, it's not just about what you know, but what you're known for. Your personal brand and reputation in industry are important to your progression to more senior leadership roles.

What is your specific niche and what further specialised expertise do you want to develop? Can you demonstrate your established competencies through industry recognised accreditations or certifications?

Do you have a sponsor at the senior leadership level? If you've had mentors in the past, do you need a different mentor to help take you to the next level?

FOR AMBASSADORS

What do you want your legacy to be? How will the difference you've made endure beyond your working life?

You may be stepping into leadership roles outside the core industry that you've worked in. You may be crossing sectoral and geographic boundaries and this requires an extra level of political awareness and the ability to navigate a complex landscape.

Who do you rely on to support you through these challenges? Do you have a trusted sounding board who can help you maintain a clear focus and a balanced approach through uncertain times?

Consider your options carefully, use my workbook (available using the QR code on the next page) to help you choose the path that is right for you, and define your own success.

WORKBOOK

Use this QR code to download your career planning workbook:

WORK WITH MONIQUE

Monique is passionate about empowering leaders in asset management with the skills and resources they need to define their own success.

Monique offers individual coaching and mentoring for asset management professionals who want to take their careers to the next level. Working together over a 12-month period allows you to set goals and to develop and implement a plan to achieve them, with one-on-one support and guidance from Monique.

Monique also provides training and group coaching for asset management teams. These programs enable your team to lift its leadership capacity, to engage with a broad range of stakeholders and to improve your influence both inside and outside your organisation. The 12-month programs include training workshops, group coaching for your team and one-on-one mentoring for the team leader.

**To find out more about working with Monique,
visit moniquebeedles.com
or email connect@moniquebeedles.com**

TABLES AND FIGURES

Table 1: Asset management career stages 25
Table 2: Focus areas at each career stage 28
Table 3: Leadership assets required at every stage. 37
Table 4: A fixed versus growth approach. 125

Figure 1: Four stages of career development 14
Figure 2: The smarts you need to succeed. 29
Figure 3: A holistic model for value creation 123
Figure 4: Three ways to identify opportunities 125
Figure 5: Components of S&P 500 Market Value 2020 129
Figure 6: Idea to impact 132

Printed in Australia
AUHW011330060622
364644AU00002B/2